LA PLATA MOUNTAINS

Comprehensive Guide to Peaks and Trails

Debra Van Winegarden
and Thomas Holt Ward

First paperback edition, 2024

ISBN: 979-8-218-36517-2
Library of Congress Control Number: 2024903217

Published by
HIGH PLACES PRESS
Durango, Colorado
high.places.press@gmail.com

All photographs credited to the authors unless otherwise noted.

Included in this book are portions of illustrations of the
La Plata range, done from Hesperus Mountain in 1875, as part of the
Hayden Expedition to the San Juan Mountains.
They were drawn by W. H. Holmes.

This book is dedicated to

Dwight Garrigues Lavender

whose early enthusiasm for the mountains of southwest Colorado
inspired his own efforts to publish a guide to their exploration –
an enterprise sadly cut short by polio at the age of twenty-three, in 1934.

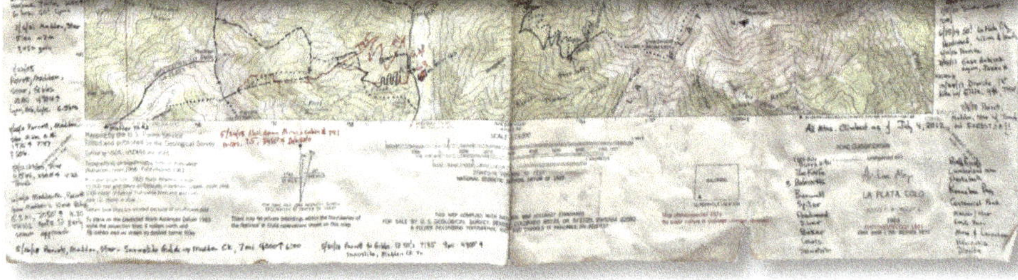

Mountain hiking and climbing are high-risk activities.
Your safety is your responsibility. The information contained in this book is based upon the experiences of the authors and might not be perceived as accurate by other persons. The safeness of the routes will likely change over time. This book is intended for use by hikers and climbers who have the requisite conditioning, experience, and common sense. High Places Press and authors do not assume any liability for injury or death, damage to property, or violation of the law that may result from the use of this book.

TABLE OF CONTENTS

Preface VII
How to Use This Guide IX
Introduction to the La Plata Mountains XIX

HIKERS

Indian Trail Ridge: from Kennebec Pass Trailhead 3
Kennebec Peak (12,101') 9
Sharkstooth Trail: Kennebec Pass Trailhead to Sharkstooth Pass 15
Burro Mountain (11,580'), the Northern Summit 21
Cumberland Mountain (12,388'), Eastern Approach 27
Olga Little Mountain (11,426') 35
Helmet Peak (11,969') to Rush Basin 41

ADVENTURERS

Centennial Peak (13,062') via Sharkstooth Trail 49
Diorite Peak (12,761') via Tomahawk Basin 55
Bald Knob (11,637'), the Eastern Summit 61
Baker Peak (11,949') via Eagle Pass 67
Silver Mountain (12,496') and Deadwood Mountain (12,285') 73
Madden Peak (11,972') and Parrott Peak (11,857'), Western Approach . 81
Four Peak Traverse: Madden, Parrott, Star, and Gibbs 87
Burwell Peak (12,664') via Boren Basin 95
Baldy Peak (10,866') from Dry Creek 101

MOUNTAINEERS

Hesperus Mountain (13,238') 111
Mount Moss (13,192') and Lavender Peak (13,237') 119
East Babcock Peak (13,149') via Tomahawk Basin 127
Middle Babcock Peak (13,161') via Boren Creek Basin 131
Spiller Peak (13,123') via Rush Basin 139
Lewis Mountain (12,740') and Snowstorm Peak (12,511') 143
Sharkstooth Peak (12,462') 151
The Knife: West Babcock Peak (13,100') to Spiller Peak (13,132') .. 157

Acknowledgements 169
About the Authors 171
Index 173

PREFACE

This guidebook is the manifestation of our devotion to the La Plata Mountains. In it we share our love for the compact range tucked in the southwest corner of Colorado. The peaks, and not just those over 13,000 feet high, are visible from all reaches of the Four Corners. They naturally elicit a compelling fascination for residents, people passing through the American West, and thru-hikers on the Colorado Trail.

The desire to explore the range is perhaps strongest for topophiles who look upon the mountains every day—your home ground. We hope to launch you so that you may answer curiosities, make your own delightful discoveries, and eventually settle into the familiarity that derives from an embedded landscape. For those who wish to deepen a sense of place, we introduce you to the human and natural history.

There is ample opportunity within the La Plata Mountains to satisfy hikers and climbers of all abilities. Plentiful pathways assist initial exploration of the range: trails, abandoned wagon roads, and rugged 4WD tracks. Together, they propel visitors into high basins, along ridgeline traverses, and even to the crest of some peaks. The established treadways described within this guide will satisfy most hikers.

For those of you who haven't hiked unless you've climbed a mountain, there are twenty-six to choose from—seventeen ranked peaks and nine named points. The majority of summits are approached off-trail. We have explored most feasible routes. We've returned over and again to hone the most elegant and safest lines to each prominence. However, there are many ways to climb a mountain. While this guide is comprehensive in its peak coverage, other routes await your discovery.

Our deepest intention is to help you find your way there and back safely. The guide is arranged simply. We begin with the easiest hike and close with the most difficult. Please start at the beginning and advance only as far as your fitness, experience, and skills permit.

This guidebook is the outcome of a quarter century of concentrated exploring and mountaineering in the La Platas. I began probing deeply into the range through long-distance runs and solo summit climbs in 2000. I kept detailed field notes about my favorite lines and those I marked "Don't Repeat!" I hand-drew routes on the USGS La Plata topographical map. I partnered with Tomás in 2010 and together we climbed my twenty-sixth summit in 2012, Bald Knob.

With technical support from Tomás, in 2014, I started the blog, Earthline:

The American West. While its current mission is to document observations of the landscape in the Four Corners region, its initial intent was simply to describe routes up all the peaks in the La Plata range. Readers requested a guidebook that could be carried. Together, Tomás and I began actively working on the guide in March, 2020 during the Covid Pandemic lockdown.

As we got deeper into the project we needed better photographs, GPX tracks, and tighter route descriptions for some peaks. Over three years we re-climbed many of the prominences, including nearly all of the summits in the Mountaineers section.

Perhaps the La Platas are in your backyard. Maybe you walked clear across the state and are finishing your journey among these peaks. Or, you are climbing all the thirteeners in the San Juan Mountains. Whatever the nature of your quest, we are honored to share with you the joys we've experienced over the years in the La Plata Mountains.

Debra Van Winegarden
Durango, March, 2023

HOW TO USE THIS GUIDE

A quick review of my own bookshelf reveals that there are at least as many ways to provide instructions for getting from point A to point B as there are guides resting there. Each has its strengths and weaknesses, its own character and feel.

Here we have tried to avoid what we find cumbersome or annoying and favor the clear and enlightening. The result is a combination of features which should be familiar to those well acquainted with this section of the library, along with an addition or two of our own.

Some readers will hopefully never even read this chapter, having found our choices so brilliantly intuitive, no explanation is required. For the rest, read on.

Organization Into Three Sections

Overall, the hikes proceed from easier to harder from the front cover to the back. They seemed to us to be distinctly divisible into three types, so we have divided the book into three sections, which we have titled:

Hikers	These hikes do not require any scrambling (although some have options). They are less strenuous and involve less challenging surfaces (some are still off-trail however) and are not scary at all.
Adventurers	These hikes may involve minor scrambling, are all fairly strenuous, and some of them involve significant exposure.
Mountaineers	All of these are challenging in every way, being strenuous, dangerous, and even hard to navigate. They can be done from our description alone, but it is highly recommended that you find someone with prior experience to accompany you.

One Hike, One Chapter

Each chapter describes a specific route to a specific destination. Optional related routes may also be described. In all cases, the chapter is meant to be a completely self-contained entity. We have avoided the space-saving practice of referring the reader to various other places in the book for necessary information.

So, as you progress through the book, you will notice certain instructions appearing more than once. This is by design and is particularly convenient if you are copying the chapter to take along with you. (Alternatively, bulking up your pack with heavy tomes will improve your fitness.)

Inspiration

Below the title of each chapter you will find the words of writers far more accomplished than the authors of this book. In case you were wondering what this is for, well, it is meant to inspire. Some are even especially appropriate to the adventure described, so... let that be a puzzle for you.

Below the quote there is a one-paragraph description sketching out the hike's main characteristics and attractions. This too is meant to showcase more specifically the high points of that particular experience.

As Much Detail As You Like

Every reader decides on a hike based upon their own priorities with regard to the various important characteristics of a hike. But no one wants to have to read the complete chapter in order to get an idea of what those are. Here we offer four levels of detail, starting with the purely symbolic boot across from the title, followed by a one paragraph description, followed by the stats block containing more specific details in terse format, and finally followed by the fully detailed description.

The Boot

Across from the title of each chapter, you will find this symbol (with text to remind you what it means). Many guides attempt to make some sort of estimate of the difficulty of a hike. But there are so 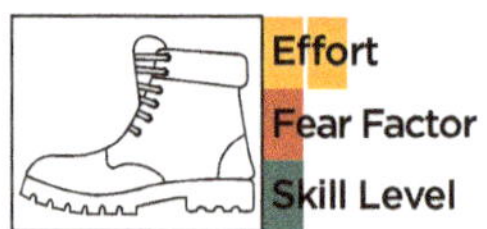

many kinds of difficulty this is often unhelpful. Instead we've divided the general notion of difficulty into three categories, which we have dubbed "Effort," "Fear Factor," and "Skill Level." There are, for example, hikes which are easy to follow and not strenuous, but involve extreme danger of a deadly fall. For some, this is no big thing, so the hike is "easy." Others might consider it so difficult as to be beyond their ability.

As a result, we have created our three compact ratings, each with a possible range from 1 through 5, as follows:

Effort	A measure of the total amount of energy required. This is a combination of the distance traveled, the elevation gained, and the types of surfaces involved. A mile is much harder over large talus than a groomed trail.
Fear Factor	Just what it sounds like, this measures the exposure to risk on the hike. This combines nearness to cliffs, steep loose terrain, and quality of holds in the rock where scrambling is involved.
Skill Level	There are multiple skills required for the hikes described here. These include climbing skills (often expressed as the class—see below), balance on steep and loose terrain, as well as the navigational skills needed for the many off-trail routes.

For example, one of the easiest hikes described, Indian Trail Ridge, is rated 2-1-1. As a very nice, relatively flat trail which is not especially long it gets a 2 for effort. Lack of any exposure to danger yields a 1 for fear, and the smooth, well signed, easily followed surface with no scrambling required ranks a 1 for skills needed.

We have not included any sort of rating for esthetics because, well, the whole range is just beautiful and spectacular and we'd have to give them all 5s.

The Stats Block

Immediately following the introductory paragraph you will find the colored, raised box titled "About This Hike." Within are listed eight key facts which define the route specifically.

Distance	Given in statute miles. This is always the round trip distance.
Elevation Gain	This is the total accumulated climbing in feet. That is to say, it counts all the ups and downs, not just the height of the peak above the trailhead.
Time	A broad estimate, mostly based on experience, again referring to the round trip time.

Route Surface	This can be a very important feature of any hike, affecting the choice of footwear, particularly. The terms used have their normal everyday meaning. All surfaces encountered during the hike will be noted regardless of their extent on the route. (Also see the glossary below.)
Class	This is the much-debated 5-level rating system. The most challenging hikes in this book do not exceed Class 4, and that is extremely rare. At least for some, this means that every hike in the book can be done without the use of protective equipment (ropes, etc.).
Exposure	The degree and amount of exposure to danger. We use a standard set of adjectives here, corresponding to the five levels in the boot: *none, mild, moderate, considerable,* and *serious.*
Navigation	Many of the destinations in this book are not graced with established trails, so there is quite a range of difficulty in finding your way. We divide this range into just three categories: *easy, moderate,* and *challenging.*
Other Maps	A single USGS 7.5' topographic map (La Plata) covers over 90 percent of the routes described. If a route does reach off the edge of that one, the appropriate additional map is indicated here.

Note that some hikes which include optional or alternate segments may show multiple values in these fields, labeled appropriately.

Travel

Here we describe as carefully as possible how not to get lost in the maze of gravel roads surrounding and penetrating the mountain range.

Finding some of these trailheads can be challenging. We have chosen to use a simple and consistent method for describing these routes. A starting point for measurement is noted, following which the exact odometer reading and turn direction is given at each decision point.

Obviously, road names and landmarks are included where available, but not everything is clearly marked. Although some of these numbers were taken down multiple times, it is still possible that your mileage may vary. Automobile odometers seem to have been left behind in the age of computer precision.

It should also be noted that, with a few exceptions, parking can be extremely limited at many trailheads. Carpooling is recommended.

The Map

With thanks to the graciousness of CalTopo LLC, a full-page map appears with each hike, integrating GPS tracks recorded on actual hikes with the 7.5' USGS topographical maps, and some helpful slope shading. Whether you like to carry paper, or use an app on your phone, or carry a purpose-built device, comparing these maps with your own navigational aid can be indispensable to finding your way successfully.

Route

The remainder of each chapter is simply the full details of how to get to your destination and what you might enjoy seeing along the way. In some cases, getting the route correct may require both the words contained here and the included topographical map. Many of the photos are just for enjoyment and basic illustration, but we have also included some specifically to help guide the hiker.

As it would be a shame to pass through this wilderness without some appreciation for its rich history, both natural and human, or the creatures that inhabit it, some few notes on these topics are included. In particular, it would be truly negligent not to give some space to the botanical kaleidoscope of wildflowers that so generously decorate your path.

Terminology

Experienced hikers, perhaps especially those who like to hike in groups, will find nothing mysterious here. However, not everyone uses terms in exactly the same way, nor do we wish to put off the uninitiated with jargon. Here's a short list of a few sometimes-ambiguous terms and the precise meanings we assign them herein.

Class
In mountaineering, whether it be scrambling, bouldering, rock climbing, or alpine ascents, this is a measure of difficulty of the terrain. There is a lot of wiggle room on these definitions, but here's a quick summary:

1 Sidewalk to smooth trail.
2 Walking off-trail on rough surfaces, but not requiring handholds.
3 Climbing requiring the use of hands to make progress.
4 Class 3 with greater verticality and exposure and more limited holds.
5 Even more limited holds and greater exposure than Class 4 and therefore sufficiently dangerous to require the use of protective equipment (ropes and anchors).

exposure
Perhaps this is just short for "exposure to danger." More specifically it refers to both the amount and the degree of risk on a route.

friable rock
With reference to scrambling situations, this is rock that fractures, crumbles, or cleaves off easily, often in spite of appearing to be perfectly solid.

jeep track
Or sometimes two-track, this refers to routes that were actual roads once upon a time, but no longer allow vehicle traffic. They are sometimes even difficult to imagine as roads, but often appear on old topographic maps.

out-and-back
A route which goes to a destination and returns by the same path.

Point 1,234'
Topographic maps often mark prominences with an altitude. If the prominence does not qualify for peak status, then it is referred to in this way, where 1,234' is the marked altitude.

Peak 1,234'   As above, except that the prominence does qualify for peak status, but lacks a name.

scrambling   This is a term for climbing through rock using hands and feet to make progress. In terms of Class this might refer to classes 2+ through 4, but mostly Class 3.

stem-and-loop   A route which has a loop at the end of an out-and-back section (the stem). The stem is at the trailhead end.

social trail   An unofficial trail which is nonetheless clearly visible due simply to the frequency of use by hikers.

talus   An expanse of fragmented rocks or boulders absent any significant vegetation. These are found throughout the La Platas, frequently on the hillsides near the summits, but they can be anywhere. The bigger the blocks, the slower the going.

trail   We reserve this term for constructed and/or official trails.

wildcat trail   Similar to social trail, except that it implies something less frequently used, or even improper (such as one that cuts across private property).

After reading this, one might reasonably ask what actually makes a summit a "peak?" By long-time convention, at least in Colorado, a prominence is considered a peak if it rises at least 300 vertical feet above the saddle separating it from any neighboring peak.

In recent years, the USGS has been involved in creating a completely new altitude map of the United States based on LiDAR (light detection and ranging). Due to the high accuracy (4 inches) of this technique, there have been many updates to the altitudes listed on topographical maps. While this effort is ongoing, we have generally used the values on the old topo maps with a few exceptions for the highest peaks, where there has been some controversy about their actual heights.

Preparedness and Safety

"Mountains are not fair or unfair, they are just dangerous."
— Reinhold Messner

The wisdom of the legendary climber is probably as good a disclaimer as anything I've heard. Anyone undertaking treks in the wilderness, including those described here, is taking a risk no matter how well they are prepared.

That being said, the value of proper preparation cannot be overstated. It will protect you from all manner of unexpected mishaps time and again.

What to Pack

You can easily find endless lists of what you should carry with you when hiking in the wilderness. Rather than recommend a very specific list, let's consider the basic categories:

protection	This is your clothing. Footwear, hats, layers, sun protection, and rain gear should cover at least the range of expected conditions for the day. Note that in the mountains, precipitation and cold are possible in every season. It should also be noted that there is no known protection against lightning except avoidance.
navigation	The range of navigational aids, both electronic and otherwise, has never been greater. And yet, people still get lost. Make sure you learn how to correctly use whatever combination you decide on. And decide on something.
survival	This is what you need to continue functioning during the hike: food, water, medicine, and first aid. You should carry more than the minimum amount of these. In particular, a generous water ration is a good idea in spite of the weight. A headlamp is also recommended and easily included.
rescue	As of this writing, you cannot count on your cellphone to get you out of trouble in the La Platas.

Current technology does offer many alternative electronic satellite-based communication devices. Pick one. A whistle and/or flashing light can also be invaluable for attracting attention as potential rescuers search out your precise location.

How to Behave

If it is possible to summarize the proper attitude in a single word, it would be: *mindful.* There are all sorts of tips and tricks people have tabulated for staying out of trouble while trekking, but they mostly amount to just paying close attention to what you're doing.

Just the same, here are a few specific recommendations:

watch your step	Obvious, right? But this can be difficult when surrounded by the magnificence of mountain tundra in high summer. Stop frequently in admiration, but keep your eyes down on rough trails and rocky routes.
use trekking poles	Using one or two trekking poles not only aids in balance and contributes to your power, they can also save you from a painful fall if you slip. We have observed this personally innumerable times.
think ahead	The most common danger here is often phrased: don't go up what you can't come down. It is a peculiar fact of climbing that many obstacles can be ascended easily enough, but are impossible to descend. Less commonly, the reverse can also be true.
	This rule also applies with regard to navigation. Off-trail, things can look very different traveling in opposite directions. Alway look back and take note of how your route will look on the return.

A final observation on rescue. The two most valuable approaches to this are still probably the oldest: don't hike alone and leave word with a responsible person about your destination and expected return.

A Note About Navigation

Very often the most crucial element of navigation is simply knowing in which direction you are walking. This is particularly true if you are lost and trying to find your way back.

You might be aware, for example, that if you can simply keep progressing to the west, you will eventually encounter a known road. Assuming your only remaining instrument is a time piece, and you can locate the sun in the sky, the following simple truth might be helpful.

The sun's position in the sky tracks the time of day in a manner that is absolutely consistent regardless of the season. In the northern hemisphere, the sun is directly east at 6 am, directly south at noon, and directly west at 6 pm. (You might have to subtract an hour to correct for daylight saving time.) Interpolating for five of the eight points of the compass, this becomes: 6 am-E, 9 am-SE, 12-S, 3 pm-SW, and 6 pm-W. These are only rough headings, but as it is generally impossible to walk a straight line in the wilderness, they are pretty much as good as is useful, and they will prevent you from walking in circles.

Leave No Trace

The La Plata Mountains have in recent times benefitted much from neglect. One of the great attractions of wandering its dramatic peaks and peaceful basins is, in fact, the solitude it offers. As a result, it has not suffered the damage brought on by too much love from the hiking community. The highest peaks have been blessed with a small inadequacy in altitude, failing to attain a certain much-sought-after round number.

If only the same could be said of its treatment during the mining years. Today, some of the decaying structures of those efforts have a certain charm, but the same cannot be said of the iridescent outflows from old adits after a strong rain. Leave the ruins as they are, but please lend your financial and political support to any effort to plug the toxic leaks.

So much the more must we be vigilant in preserving this isolated wonder. We urge all who venture here: leave beauty as you found it, and where you see others' trash left sadly behind, collect and remove it.

Together we can do better than just preserve; we can restore.

INTRODUCTION TO THE LA PLATA MOUNTAINS

*In many respects this is a very remarkable group of mountains.
Occupying an area not more than ten miles square, and being situated in
the remote southwest, almost isolated from the great mountain chains, it
yet has a number of lofty summits which fall but little short of 14,000 feet
elevation. A cluster of these, which lie just north of the head of the La Plata
River, are among the most rugged and picturesque mountains in Colorado.*
— William H. Holmes, 1875

Little has changed in the century-plus that has elapsed since Holmes, a talented geologist of the Hayden Expedition, first laid eyes on this place. The stamp mills are quiet now and barely any trace remains of Parrott City, which housed the workers of a bustling industry at that time. Those who seek out its challenges and beauty today tread far more gently.

As the lead geologist of the expedition to southwest Colorado, Holmes mapped in detail the topography and geology of the La Platas. As it happens, he was also an extraordinary sketch artist, a skill that served well the reports he made as part of his official role. That he was moved to draw a stunning panoramic of the mountain range as seen from its highest point speaks to a little more than his sense of duty. While we cannot do justice to the complete chromolithographic image here, we have used selections from it to grace the backgrounds of the three section title pages.

So, then, appropriate to both this little anecdote and the natural timeline, let us begin our own verbal sketch with Holmes's particular focus.

NATURAL HISTORY

Geology

The story of this mountain range, like the stories of many other things on earth, both living and mineral, starts at the bottom of the sea.

In this case, it was a wide, shallow inland passage known as the Cretaceous Sea. Its shores moved back and forth over dozens of millions of years, and layers of alternating marine and terrestrial sediments were laid to thicknesses of thousands of feet.

It was in this context, about 75 million years ago, during a period of submersion, that the drama of birth began for our range. A mass of molten earth began slowly but insistently rising from beneath the ancient sediments. A great dome rose gently from the sea, straining the hard sediments with fissures and cracks into which the magma oozed, cooking and transforming the ancient layers and swelling this new amalgam even more. Over the next five million years or so, this dome rose many thousands of feet above the waters, the pressure from below ebbing and flowing until at last, without ever actually reaching the surface, the last finger of magma cooled and our mountain range was born.

The ocean at last receded while the weathering of the overlying sediments began. Wind, water and ice cut away at the softest and most fractured places. Even glaciers had their turn at carving up large masses of rock until the harder material of the intruded plutonic mass was exposed. Eventually, the current topography took shape, the highest places now dominated by the once invisible molten invader. Mountain ranges that are formed in this way are called laccoliths in the science of stone, and the La Platas are considered a classic example.

Of course, as some say, geology never sleeps and this landscape will continue its journey. But this is where we come into the story. Humans, that is. And, as usual, our presence will get a most unfair amount of attention by comparison to the life-cycle of mountains.

In fact, it is worth remembering that the complete human history to date here is almost literally a blink of an eye compared to the glacial timescales of rock. So, when you look across the valley at a spectacular cliff or find an appealing sunny nook beneath a huge boulder, recall that it is entirely likely that every human who has ever passed that way has admired that same cliff, possibly even sat in that same nook to rest.

Much of what the explorer into this realm will see is defined by this story of slow-motion geological violence. Perhaps most obvious of all are the clearly banded cliffs of Centennial and Hesperus, where the layers of cooked sediment and igneous intrusion are displayed in strong contrasts of color.

Long before humans, the rugged high country brought game looking for rich summer grazing and protection. In time this brought human hunters. The magma brought mineral wealth and miners, and that brought immigrants and settlers. Eventually, the challenges and beauty of the alpine environment attracted climbers and hikers, the audience for this guide.

We will explore these things in the following sections, but it is all

The alternating layers of sedimentary and intrusive igneous rock are clearly visible on Hesperus Mountain.

ultimately informed by the geological origin of the place.

As for the future of the story we can't know the details but we do know the end. As the earth's primal heat slowly vanishes into space, and its store of radioactive elements all eventually cool in their final half-life, only the forces of erosion will remain. No new mountains will be born, and all the glorious high places of Earth will lie spread out upon the bottom of a vast shallow sea. For the La Platas, it will be a homecoming.

Life Zones

Before the relatively recent arrival of humans, the environment of this area had become something very much like what you see today. As with many areas in Colorado, the great variations in altitude that occur even in small areas create equally diverse conditions for the plants and animals that live there.

This has led to a division of the environment by altitude into "life zones." In our area of interest, the altitude ranges from around 8,000 feet to the top of Hesperus above 13,000 feet. This range is covered by the highest three zones:

Montane
This zone, at elevations of 8,000 to 9,500 feet, is where you find Colorado natives ponderosa pine, Douglas fir, lodgepole pine, and aspen growing in thick forests.

Subalpine
At 9,500 to 11,500 feet dense forests of subalpine fir and Engelmann spruce are the dominant native trees.

Alpine
Above timberline at 11,500 feet and higher, this zone is made up of hardy native grasslands called tundra.

Wildlife

All the large ruminants – elk, mule deer, moose, mountain goat, and bighorn sheep – are native to the area. In modern times, however, while mule deer are frequently spotted throughout the range, you will be lucky to see any of the others. But keep an eye out. In summer, elk and bighorn are attracted to the grasses of the alpine zone where your chance of spotting them at a distance is greatly improved.

Other common large mammals include coyote and black bear. There are also certainly cougars on the prowl, but they are notoriously expert at avoiding observation by those they might prey upon (including us).

Smaller animals of interest include the ubiquitous alpine groundhog, the marmot. Beware the marmot's appetite for wire insulation. Too many have made a meal of chewing automotive wiring at high altitude trailheads, even to the point of stranding the motorist.

Also, if you are lucky, you might catch sight of the smaller, and much more shy pika. Looking rather adorably like a mouse with a heavy fur coat, they are actually more closely related to rabbits (and have no tail). You will often hear their short squeaks as you traverse their preferred rocky habitats at the highest altitudes.

Vegetation

The flora of the La Platas is, of course, very much like that of the greater San Juan Mountains of which it is a part and many books have been written on that subject. For the hiker, though, we will point out just a few things of particular interest.

Aspen	It is impossible to conceive of this mountain range without its aspen forests. These are spread throughout the area but are particularly dense on the western flank. There are numerous remarkable things to note about these trees. First, the species found in the American West are known as quaking aspen because of the way the leaves tremble in the lightest breeze, making them seem to move of their own volition.
	They grow in clonal groves where many apparently individual trees are actually growing from the same root system. The largest known grove of this type is nearby in southern Utah. It covers more than 100 acres, weighs more than 6,000 tons, and is possibly 80,000 years old, making it the largest and oldest living organism on earth.
	In the fall the leaves turn almost simultaneously, across huge areas, to their characteristic brilliant gold, sometimes with just a blush of red here and there. It is a common practice to hike the peaks of the western block during autumn for this reason alone.
	Finally, the specific character of the smooth bark and how the trees heal wounds to that bark have made it a canvas for the graffiti of the passers-by of the ages. (See the Four Peak Traverse chapter for an example.) Since the individual trunks can last as long as 200 years, we have seen many arborglyphs (as they are called) documenting the presence of miners of the early 20th century. As charming as

some of these old inscriptions are, we recommend refraining from making your own additions. Modern pressure upon these forests requires more restraint than once was the case.

Tundra

The wondrous expanses of smooth and brilliant green that carpet the alpine regions constitute a destination in themselves. While the range is not particularly noted for alpine meadows, it does possess them in plenty. The hike to Silver Mountain via Deadwood, for example, traverses miles of tundra along an airy alpine ridge.

The tundra is, however, a delicate beauty. There are no legal restrictions on where you walk up there, but we encourage all hikers to follow routes consistently and use whatever trails, however faint, that they find in these areas. Treading lightly is most important here.

As for the Colorado tundra itself, it is an island habitat, isolated from all others like it since before the last Ice Age. The closest relatives of much of the flora still lives only far away in Siberia. Likewise, some of its insects and birds are only found in a few other places in North America, such as remote areas of Wyoming and Canada.

Wildflowers

In compiling this guide it was difficult not to fill many pages with photographs of alpine and subalpine wildflowers. If there is anyone reading this who has not experienced this aspect of the Colorado high country in summer, then I would recommend buying an identification guide before venturing out. It will add to your enjoyment of the cornucopia.

The first wildflowers, late in spring, will sometimes literally push up through the snow in June. Notable amongst the earlier risers is the aptly named glacier lily, which is often found in abundance on the watery downslope edge of melting snowbanks. (See the Kennebec Peak chapter for a photo.)

In terms of variety and abundance, the season generally peaks in mid-July. However, as each prefers its own climate window, the very progress of the season may be tracked in the colors and shapes of those most particular varieties. Who cannot feel a touch of sadness when the first pale speckled arctic gentians arrive to witness the passing of autumn in the red-tinged tundra high above treeline? (See the chapter on the Sharkstooth Trail for a photo.)

And one final note of caution. Beware of the lovely flower with the macabre moniker: elegant death camas. Every part of this plant is very poisonous, causing severe illness and even death in rare cases. Be particularly cautious to keep your dogs away from this one. (See the chapter on Centennial Peak for a photo.)

HUMAN HISTORY

Prehistoric Inhabitants

Native Americans have probably frequented this mountain range for as long as 10,000 years, although little evidence of their prehistoric presence exists today. An archaic hunting blind has been identified just east of Kennebec Pass at high elevation, so we know the area has been used for hunting from the time of the earliest human visitors.

The rock shelters of the Basketmaker people have been found at the lowest elevations in the area, especially on the far eastern flank of the range (Falls Creek). Their presence is evidenced from around 0 to CE 750.

The Ancestral Puebloans followed, leaving behind the spectacular ruins of nearby Mesa Verde, but mostly living at elevations below those of our mountains. However, oral traditions of the modern Puebloan tribes (Hopi and Zuni) indicate that the high elevations were accessed by these groups as well, probably for the hunting and gathering.

An extended and severe drought seems to have driven these groups away by around 1300.

Historic Native Americans

After 1300, and up until the arrival of the first Europeans from Spain in 1540, the extremely successful Ute tribes moved into the mountains of Colorado. Their hunter gatherer culture adapted well and their presence in the La Platas was documented by the first Spanish explorers.

The Navajo are historically known to have arrived during this same time period, settling to the south of the Utes in Colorado and into New Mexico. They often warred with Utes along the boundaries of the two cultures, which passed near to, and probably sometimes directly across the range.

Hesperus Mountain is the high point of the La Plata Mountains. In Navajo culture it is known as the sacred mountain of the north. Along with three other high peaks, it marks off the boundaries of their enormous traditional territory. Their name for the mountain, Dibe'nsta, means "Big Sheep Mountain," once again calling attention to the presence of valuable game. To this day, medicine men come to Hesperus to collect soil, rocks, and plants to use in their most sacred rituals.

Early Westerners

After 1540, the Spanish began subjugating the native inhabitants. In a rare twist to the sad story of abuse in the conquering of North America, though, there was a successful revolt against them in 1680.

This was followed by a rapid transformation of native culture through the trading of horses and guns with other Europeans not allied with the Spanish. By 1740, Southwest Colorado faced a fierce force of armed, mounted, and highly motivated Utes and Navajos. During this period, the Spanish were driven almost entirely out of the area, holding the line only as far north as Abiquiu, New Mexico.

Curiously, many of the familiar Spanish names associated with Southwest Colorado were not yet in common use. During a period of truce between the Utes and the Spanish, an expedition was launched from Abiquiu to look for silver, led by Juan Maria Antonia Rivera in 1765. Trade with the Utes included silver from the La Platas and the Spanish were anxious to investigate its source.

This expedition named most of the rivers they encountered, including the Animas, Florida, San Juan, Dolores, etc. Although they did not record La Plata as the name of the river draining our mountain range, it was a specific goal of the expedition to explore that river and its watershed for silver. It is exceedingly likely that they named the La Plata River as well, but the recording of this fact was lost to history. (The entire record of the expedition, in fact, was very nearly lost to history.) In time the mountain range that feeds the river probably simply took on the name as well.

The expedition, however, was deemed unsuccessful with regard to silver, and almost another century would pass before the invasion of men seeking precious metals would begin in earnest.

Used by permission of the Animas Museum, Durango, CO

John Moss looking as dapper and sophisticated as he was described by his contemporaries.

Mining

Unfortunately for the original inhabitants, the Spanish were not the end of the encroachment on their territory by Euro-Americans. By the mid-1800s, the wealth of the San Juans had been discovered by the westward migration of citizens of a rapidly expanding United States.

The earliest significant attempt to exploit the deposits of the La Platas came from "Captain" John Moss (the title is thought to have been honorary). Moss was a very unusual character. Described as "courtly," "witty," and "well-educated," he is also rumored to have spoken Ute. In 1873 he made a deal with Chief Ignacio to farm and mine in a 36-square-mile area along the La Plata River near the mouth of La Plata Canyon. A town was set up on the site.

He received funding for his venture through a San Francisco financier named Tiburcio Parrott. In recognition of this he named his town Parrott City. In time, the prominence overlooking the settlement also became known as Parrott Peak.

The town prospered rapidly and became the La Plata county seat in 1876 when Colorado became a state. Unfortunately, the placer mines that the operation was meant to exploit played out quickly. The town continued to exist for some time based on farming and ranching, but Parrott withdrew his financial support and John Moss returned to California permanently. He made an impression on the Hayden Expedition, however, and Mount Moss now bears his name. The town slowly died out, becoming a ghost town with the last remnant, the Barbee Hotel, burning down in 1963.

By the time the placer mines failed, the more profitable hard-rock veins of the nearby mountains had been discovered and were being actively prospected.

Even before Moss's arrival, the US government decided to conduct proper geological survey and mapping expeditions of the newly declared Colorado Territory. A series of these were launched under the guidance of F. V. Hayden. One in particular came to the La Platas in 1875 with geologist William Holmes, whose words introduced this chapter. The results of that survey provided rich material for prospectors and helped accelerate the exploitation of the mountains.

Apart from Moss's surprisingly peaceful interaction with the Native Americans, this was a time of deadly conflict. Much is written about the multiple treaties that were signed, broken, re-written, and signed again, but the story is easily summarized. The number, power, and greed of the new migrants eventually overwhelmed the Utes. Having once inhabited all of what is now Colorado, they were finally forced into the small area that they now inhabit. The Navajo fared no better, and their sacred mountain no longer rests on their own land.

It is perhaps a small consolation to us all that much of this land, including nearly all of the La Platas, now belongs to the public, which at least includes the progeny of its original caretakers.

Mining continued for decades in the La Platas, even well into the 20th century. While it was productive, no great fortunes were made, and mining eventually became less profitable as the most accessible veins played out. In spite of the name, it is estimated that, in the end, the most valuable extraction was that of gold rather than silver.

Recreational Use

The final wave of visitors to arrive here brings us up to date with the state of things as they are today. The outdoor enthusiast now clearly dominates the landscape. Hunters, campers, hikers, and climbers take advantage of its wild game, scenic beauty, and climbing challenges. There is even a kind of niche tourism that interests itself in the environmentally regrettable, but nonetheless fascinating ruins of the mining industry.

Hunting, of course, has been part of its history since the arrival of humans. But amongst the others the first was probably the climber.

Undoubtedly, the Native Americans climbed many (probably all) of these peaks long before the arrival of Europeans, but we know nothing of that history. It is also possible that some of these peaks were climbed by the Spaniards in the 16th and 17th centuries, but there is no clear record of that, either.

By the time the first Department of the Interior survey teams arrived with the Hayden Expedition in 1875, they recorded that many of the La Plata peaks had been climbed by the earliest miners looking for rich outcrops, many of which are most visible along the highest ridges.

Following them closely, the first surveyors were perhaps the most impressive, not only climbing the peaks, but doing so carrying the tools of the trade: tripod-mounted theodolite, bulky camera, and cistern barometer. Gibbs and Burwell peaks are both named for surveyors. The Hayden Expedition to the La Platas selected a number of its members specifically for their climbing ability.

They are also responsible for the modern name of the high point of the range. Thinking Hesperus Mountain was the westernmost of the high peaks of Colorado, they chose the Greek god associated with the evening star (which appears each night above the western horizon).

By the turn of the 20th century, while the stamp mills continued to grind up the innards of our laccolith, the first parties to climb Colorado's peaks purely for the pleasure of it were recorded. Both men and women are pictured in early photographs of such groups on high peaks, such as Uncompahgre. By early in the century, Colorado's exclusive collection of summits exceeding a certain round number – the "14ers" – had all been climbed. It seems that the popularity of the mountains on this list has only grown over the past hundred-plus years.

Around 1920, the first of the alpine mountaineers trained in European technique arrived in Colorado. One in particular, Albert R. Ellingwood, attacked the most difficult peaks with enthusiasm, scoring numerous first ascents, including what is still considered Colorado's most difficult summit: Lizard Head.

For the southern San Juans, and the La Platas in particular, another character came on the scene in 1929. Dwight Lavender, who had grown up in Telluride, founded a loose collection of climbing enthusiasts called The San Juan Mountaineers. Like Ellingwood, the group did not restrict themselves to just the 14ers, rather pursuing anything and everything of interest, looking in particular for new summits and new routes to familiar ones.

A meticulous chronicler of these exploits, Lavender compiled one of the earliest climbing guides to the San Juans, and certainly the earliest guide to the La Platas. The type-written manuscript, entitled The San Juan Mountaineers' Climber's Guide to Southwestern Colorado, includes his own maps and drawings, as well as photos taken by other members of the club. One chapter is dedicated entirely to the La Plata peaks. Compatriots Mel Griffiths and Carleton Long contributed significantly as well.

Unfortunately, possibly because of his tragic early death from polio in 1934 at age 23, the work was never published. Lavender had made the fateful decision to return to his college work at Stanford University where he contracted the fatal disease. A few copies exist in special collections in

Used by permission of the University of Colorado, Boulder, CO

Dwight Lavender demonstrating the proper rappelling technique of the time.

Colorado libraries, however, and make for fascinating reading.

One of Lavender's climbing partners in those early days was Thomas Melvin (Mel) Griffiths. Mel lived a long and productive life, and in the 1970s decided to honor his old friend and pioneer climber of San Juan peaks. He sent a proposal to the appropriate agency to attach Dwight's name to an unnamed 13er in the La Platas. The proposal was accepted in 1976, and Lavender Peak now bears his surname. As we consider it our favorite summit, often combined with an ascent of Mount Moss, we find this both satisfying and appropriate.

At this point in the story, the scene has been set for our range as it exists today. Along with its designation as public land have come multiple campgrounds both in La Plata Canyon and on its western flank above Mancos. Hiking, horseback riding, and four-wheeling have come along as other means of enjoying the back country.

The popularity of camping and hiking in the range has probably never been greater. And yet, it remains for the most part a kind of locals' paradise. Climbing the summits described here is almost always a private, even intimate, experience. And that is certainly one of its greatest charms.

Public Lands

President Theodore Roosevelt created the San Juan National Forest in 1905. With the exception of some private in-holdings in La Plata Canyon, the La Plata Mountains remain entirely within it, preserved in their more or less natural state in perpetuity.

As a user of this incomparable resource, we urge everyone to be generous and vigilant. Give money where and when you can, leave as little trace of your visits as possible, and be cognizant of the effect of your political choices on its preservation.

HIKERS

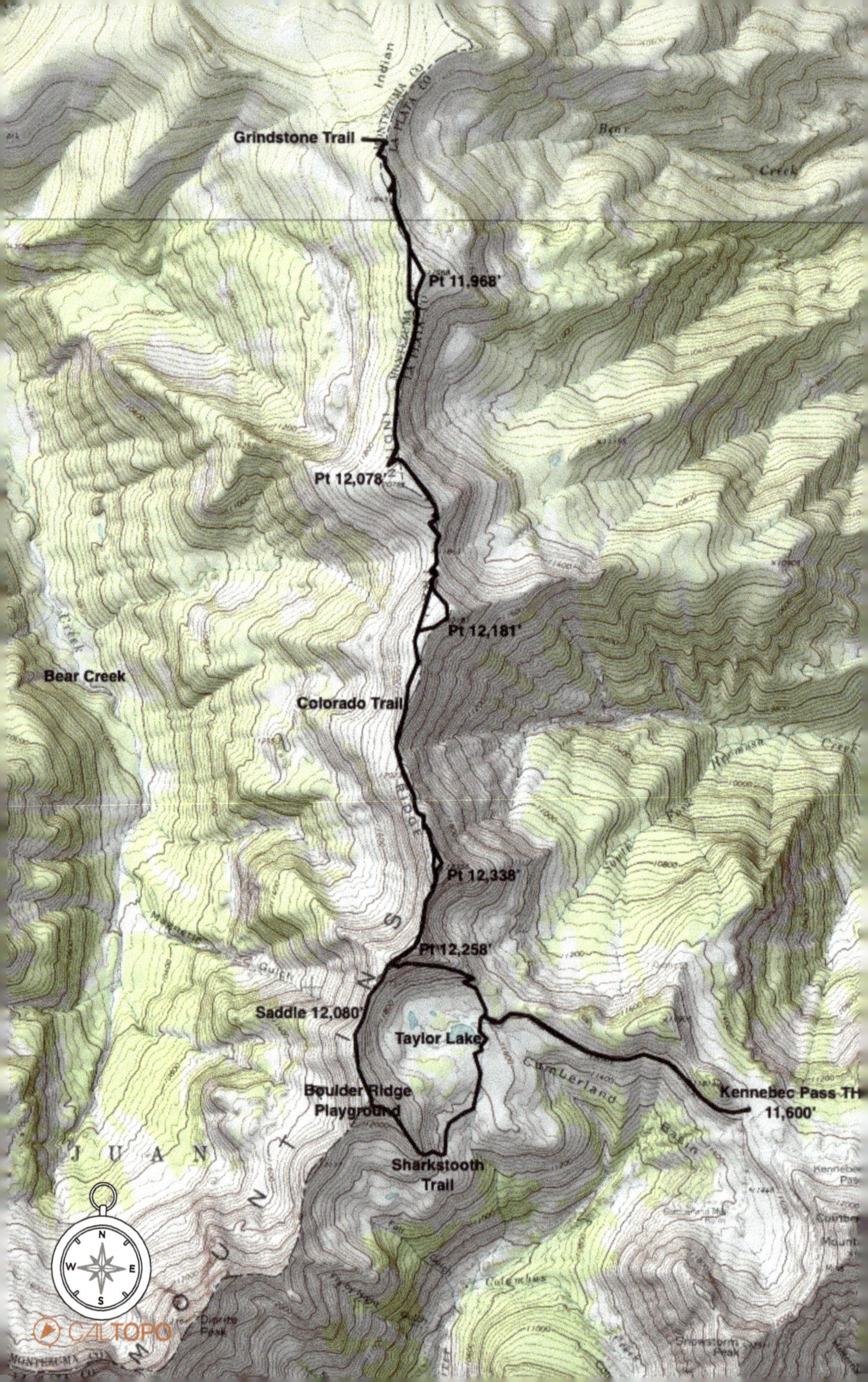

Grindstone Trail
Pt 11,968'
Pt 12,078'
Pt 12,181'
Bear Creek
Colorado Trail
Pt 12,338'
Pt 12,258'
Saddle 12,080'
Taylor Lake
Boulder Ridge Playground
Sharkstooth Trail
Kennebec Pass TH 11,600'
N
S
E
W
CALTOPO

INDIAN TRAIL RIDGE

Eastward the dawn rose, ridge behind ridge into the morning, and vanished out of eyesight into guess; it was no more than a glimmer blending with the hem of the sky, but it spoke to them, out of the memory and old tales, of the high and distant mountains.

— J.R.R. Tolkien

Indian Trail Ridge is the great alpine connector, linking the San Juan Mountains with the La Plata Range via the Colorado Trail. The diversity and abundance of wildflowers is as big and bold as the continuous panorama. Design your hike from the Kennebec Pass Trailhead. Turn around at Taylor Lake or do any portion of the out-and-back to the Grindstone Trail. Scramblers may finish with an off-trail loop through the "Boulder Playground" at the southern end of the ridge.

ABOUT THIS HIKE

Distance: 12.5 miles as described; your mileage may vary
Elevation Gain: 2,620 feet of climbing for the full hike
Time: 6:30 to 7:30
Route Surface: Colorado Trail; off-trail on ridge crest; block fields in the Boulder Playground
Class: 1 to 2+
Exposure: none
Navigation: easy

Travel

Measure distance from the junction of US 160 and La Plata Canyon Road, CR 124. After passing the hamlet of Mayday the road turns to smooth dirt at 4.6 miles. In 8.5 miles the roadbed deteriorates with sharp, sizable rocks. At 12.0 miles the road splits; take the left track, FSR 571. High clearance and 4WD is recommended from here. It is 14.0 miles to the Kennebec Pass Trailhead from US 160.

Route

A tangle of tracks and trails pin-wheel from the Kennebec Pass Trailhead at 11,600 feet. Take a moment to be certain you are heading west on the

Colorado Trail toward Taylor Lake. A popular destination, the lake is a relatively flat 1.2 miles away via a groomed singletrack.

Round to the northwest and Diorite Peak appears. The southern end of Indian Trail Ridge (ITR) cradles the lake platform. Just before the lake, the trail splits. Turn right, staying on the Colorado Trail. Grindstone Trail, the northern turn-around for this hike, is 4.5 miles from here.

Skirt the north side of the lake and begin a gradual 520-foot ascent to the ridge. The lake recedes while the East Block of the range rises to steal the show.

There are five numbered points and one ranked summit on the ITR south of the Grindstone Trail. It is a great pleasure and simply done to leave the trail and tag the high points while hiking north.

Past the first roller, Point 12,258', the ridge constricts and crosses a stone causeway. Then the trail ascends almost to the crest of softly rounded Peak 12,338'. This is the loftiest rise of the day so make every effort to heft up the extra 80 feet.

From Peak 12,338', the view from solitary Lone Cone to the Lizard Head spire is but a small slice of the horizon's unfettered circle. The crest affords an uncommon perspective on the La Plata Mountains. The arc swings from Diorite Peak to Sharkstooth Peak. Banded Hesperus Mountain, 13,238', is the tallest eminence in the range and widely regarded through-out the ages as the most noble.

Seen from Indian Trail Ridge, the high tops of the La Platas rise above Bear Creek Basin.

Miles slide by effortlessly on the immaculate Colorado Trail marked by stone monuments. The cairns seem rather superfluous on the restricted divide. And yet, these stone boys are imbued with historical and even archetypal significance. They have stood watch through the ages as native peoples, sheepherders, and cross-state backpackers have walked upon this thin and vital link between mountain ranges.

The flora throughout the hike is so rich, by mid-summer ninety percent of Colorado's wildflower inventory is in bloom. Old man of the mountain (alpine sunflower) lives in absurdly opulent conditions with his feminine companion, rosy paintbrush. He keeps house with aromatic phlox, chiming bluebells, tasty geyer onion, and mountain parsley. Horizontal slabs of stone are carelessly strewn about with arnica springing from the cracks.

Be watchful for fauna and you may see swallows at speed, curious ermine, yellow-bellied marmots, mountain lion tracks, mule deer, and large herds of elk in both the Hermosa Creek and Bear Creek drainages.

Approaching the Grindstone Trail junction, the land plummets into the darkly forested Hermosa Creek watershed. Across the rift, the sky-cleaving San Juan Mountains punctuate the earthline.

While the hike turns around here and stays on the trail for the return trip, there are options for distance hikers. The Colorado Trail continues north and just keeps on going all the way to Denver. Or, return on the 20-mile Historic Highline Loop. It was designated a National Recreation Trail in 1979 because of its extraordinary scenic value. For the loop, take the Grindstone Trail west to the Bear Creek Trail. Walk south to the junction with the Sharkstooth Trail, and then east back to Taylor Lake.

Boulder Playground

This optional loop leaves the Colorado Trail where it intersected Indian Trail Ridge. Hikers who generally stick to trails should simply return to the trailhead for a total of 11.5 miles. The Boulder Playground is suggested for experienced scramblers seeking a frolicsome adventure. Leave the trail on the east side of a willow patch and head south on the ridge to a saddle at 12,080 feet.

Hop along on stepping stones with resistant, crystalline veins. Cross a block field and then climb gently for 170 feet to the final roll of the ridge at 12,250 feet. Pass two communication towers topping the point. Where the ridge splits, descend the southeast rib and enter the jumble of stones. The rock is solid and holds are good but the enormous boulders tend to teeter totter under foot.

Intersect the Sharkstooth Trail at the southern terminus of the ITR. Turn left, pass Taylor Lake, and link back with the Colorado Trail.

An optional descent
route provides
a playground for agile
rock lovers.

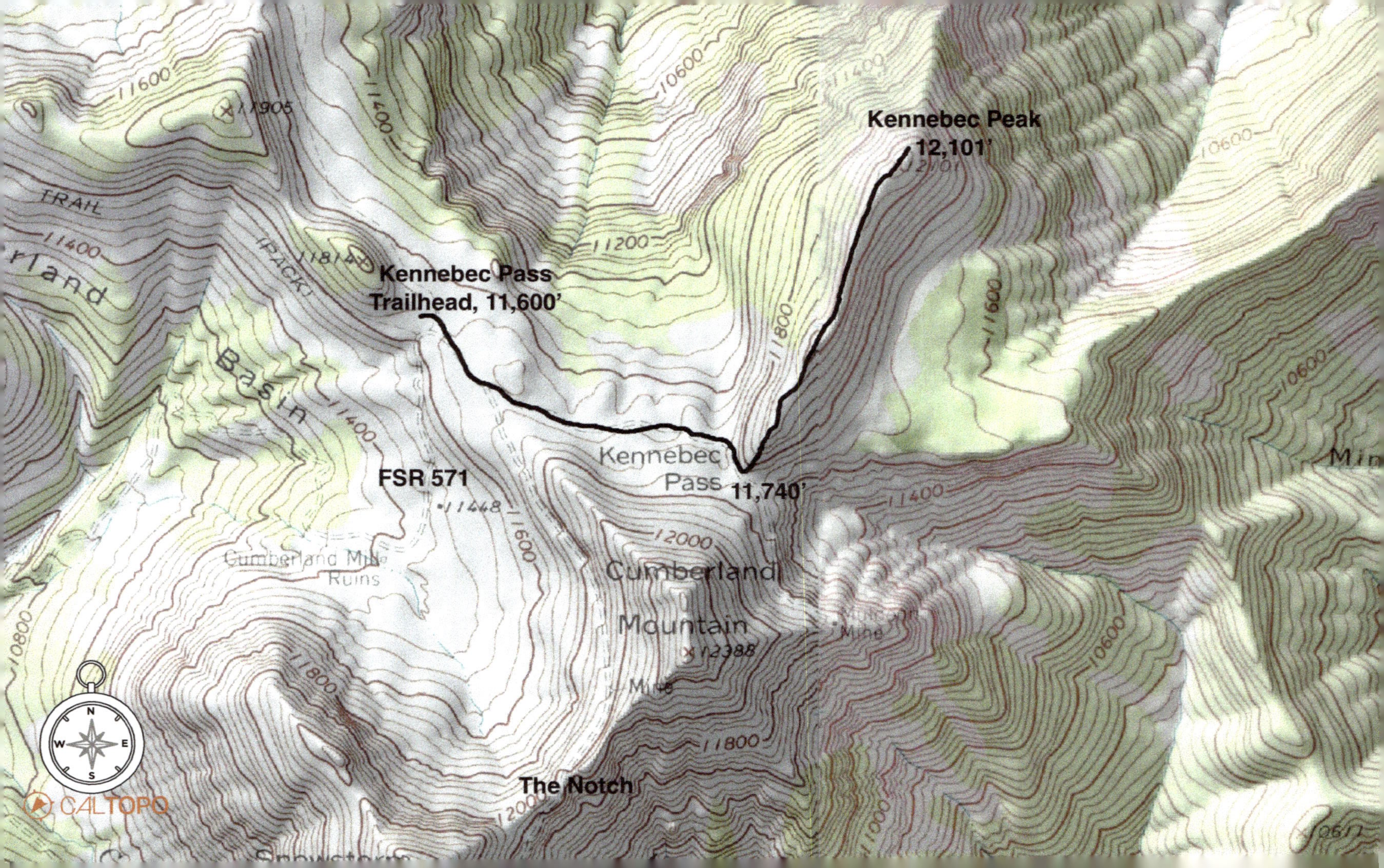
11600
11905
TRAIL
11400
Basin
11400
(PACK)
11814P
Kennebec Pass
Trailhead, 11,600'
10600
11200
11400
Kennebec Peak
12,101'
12701
10600
11800
11600
10600
FSR 571
11448
1400
1600
Kennebec
Pass 11,740'
11400
12000
Cumberland Mine Ruins
Cumberland
Mountain
12388
Mine
Mine
10800
11800
The Notch
11800
11200
10600
1000
CALTOPO
N
W   E
S

KENNEBEC PEAK, 12,101'

The temple bell stops but I still hear the sound coming out of the flowers.
— Matsuo Bashō

Peak 12,101' is the most northerly ranked summit on the East Block and the easiest mountain to scale in the range. Take a short and glorious, flower infused stroll on a rising causeway to informally named Kennebec Peak. Look across voluminous, yawning space to the San Juan Mountains. This is an ideal first mountain for young children.

ABOUT THIS HIKE
Distance: 2.8 miles
Elevation Gain: 500 feet
Time: 1:30 to 2:30
Route Surface: trail, off-trail
Class: 2
Exposure: none
Navigation: easy
Additional Map: Monument Hill, Colorado 7.5' USGS Quad

Travel

Measure distance from the junction of US 160 and La Plata Canyon Road, CR 124. After passing the hamlet of Mayday the road turns to smooth dirt at 4.6 miles. In 8.5 miles the roadbed deteriorates with sharp, sizable rocks. At 12.0 miles the road splits; take the left track, FSR 571. High clearance and 4WD are recommended from here. It is 14.0 miles to the Kennebec Pass Trailhead from US 160. This hike can be approached from the east side of Kennebec Pass via a slightly tamer road. See Cumberland Mountain for driving and hiking directions.

Route

From the Kennebec Pass Trailhead, elevation 11,600 feet, Peak 12,101' appears to the northeast as a softly rising ridge at the concluding end of the range.

Because of its strategic location right on the Colorado Trail, the trailhead is often used as a resupply station for thru-hikers. As a point of confusion

for many, Kennebec Pass proper is 0.7 mile east. While hiking to the pass, imagine how thru-hikers from Denver must savor this final high-alpine stretch of their 486-mile journey. The 4,860-foot drop from Kennebec Pass over 22 miles to trail's end is the greatest single altitude change on the cross-state trek.

The flora is a mix of willows and an astonishing array of wildflowers. Well before access roads are plowed and opened, flowers are blooming. Snow buttercups show off waxy yellow blossoms within minutes of snowmelt. Look between the surface of the ground and the bottom of the snowpack to see marsh marigolds blooming in the subnivean zone. Glacier lily and spring beauty intertwine as winter relinquishes to spring.

By mid-summer, the tundra is covered with hybridized Indian paintbrush of variegated hues and alluring queen's crown. King's crown keeps watch nearby. All too soon, come August, fringed gentian is the harbinger of the annual fading of all things bright and cheerful and the coming of autumn.

Kennebec Pass, elevation 11,740 feet, is in the saddle between Cumberland Mountain and Peak 12,101'. Leave the Colorado Trail and begin climbing north off-trail. The summit is just 0.7 mile afar and will take about 30 minutes to achieve. The initial 200 feet is rather steep and requires the biggest effort.

Follow a social trail west of the ridge through a brief, rocky section. Alternatively, scramble directly on the ridge line.

Back on the curve-top, experience the euphoria of a simple and yet extraordinary walk up a broad ridge free of obstacles. Most La Plata ridges are narrow scrambles requiring undivided attention. But here you are free to swing around for an expansive display of the West Block where the La Plata thirteeners are concentrated: Mount Moss, Lavender Peak, Hesperus Mountain, and Centennial Peak.

Look no further than the ground for tiny enchantments. It is counterintuitive but flowers in the alpine bloom early. After sleeping for most of the year, they need to get busy and take advantage of the great wash of warmth and light to blossom and ripen seed. Look about for candy tuft and

The easily climbed summit pays off richly in views of the great San Juan peaks to the north. alpine parsley, fairy candelabra and Brandegee's clover, dwarf phlox and sky pilot, purple fringe and snowball saxifrage, and, not to be over-looked, pussytoes and kittentails.

Continue a few paces past the summit to a stone bivouac. The imponderable view of just one wedge of the visible horizon begins with Lone Cone, the westernmost summit in the San Juan Mountains. Due north across folds of green velvet is Engineer Mountain, the indisputable locals' favorite. And far away in the east in the Southern San Juans is the Rio Grande Pyramid.

Return as you came. The drive to and from the trailhead will possibly take longer than the hike, an unacceptable ratio for some. If you are excited for more hiking, consider Cumberland Mountain, Olga Little Mountain, or Taylor Lake.

If your curiosity is piqued, walk southeast from the trailhead on a two-track to The Notch. It is 0.8 mile each way and adds 400 feet of climbing. The Notch is located on the saddle between Cumberland Mountain and Snow-storm Peak. It was blown out by miners to access the Bessie G Mine which produced significant gold and silver on the east slope of Snowstorm Peak. You may visit the mine by walking a half mile south on the degenerating track.

As seen from
Cumberland Mountain,
the unofficially named
Kennebec Peak rises
above the Sliderock
Trail and Kennebec
Pass.

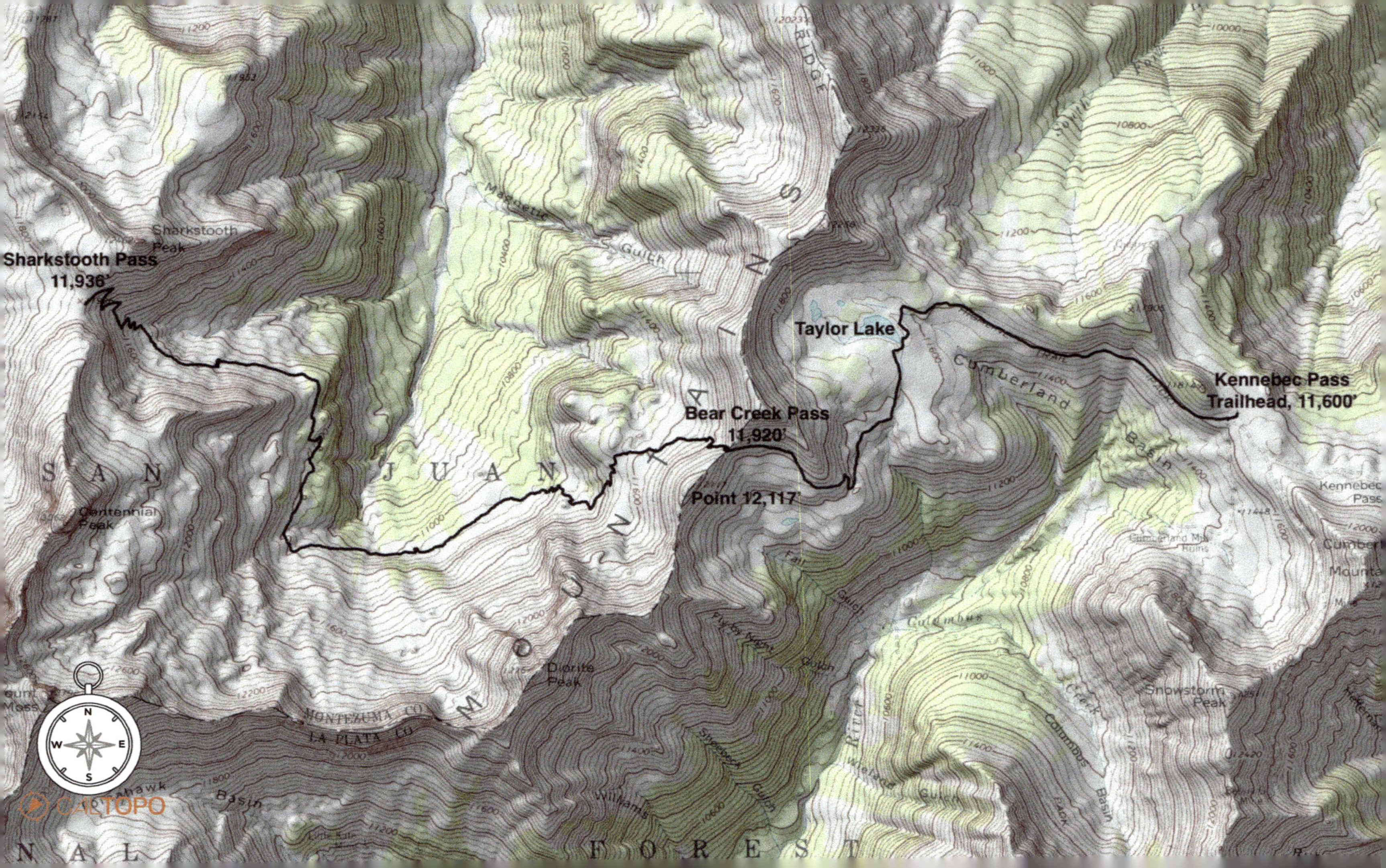
Sharkstooth Peak
Sharkstooth Pass
11,936'
Taylor Lake
Kennebec Pass
Trailhead, 11,600'
Bear Creek Pass
11,920'
Point 12,117'
Cumberland
Centennial Peak
S A N
J U A N
M O U N T A I N S
RIDGE
Kennebec Pass
Cumberland Mill Ruins
Cumberland Mountain
Basin
Columbus Basin
Snowstorm Peak
Diorite Peak
MONTEZUMA CO.
LA PLATA CO.
Williams
River
Gulch
Mohawk Basin
N A T I O N A L   F O R E S T
CARTOPO

SHARKSTOOTH TRAIL
Kennebec Pass Trailhead to Sharkstooth Pass

*As you sit on the hillside, or lie prone under the trees of the forest,
or sprawl wet-legged by a mountain stream, the great door,
that does not look like a door, opens.*

— Stephen Graham

The beautifully engineered Sharkstooth Trail spans two passes nearly identical in elevation while traversing high-basin country. Peaceful and friendly, this trail of solitude is enveloped by luxuriant, shoulder-high wildflowers and stately Engelmann spruce. Luscious water is everywhere with little waterfalls tumbling over cliffs and myriad rivulets to hop across. The out-and-back includes a segment on the Historic Highline Loop designated a National Recreation Trail in 1979 because of its extraordinary scenic value.

ABOUT THIS HIKE
Distance: 12.4 miles
Elevation Gain: 2,850 feet
Time: 5:30 to 7:00
Route Surface: trail
Class: 1
Exposure: none
Navigation: easy

Travel

Measure distance from the junction of US 160 and La Plata Canyon Road, CR 124. After passing the hamlet of Mayday the road turns to smooth dirt at 4.6 miles. In 8.5 miles the roadbed deteriorates with sharp, sizable rocks. At 12.0 miles the road splits; take the left track, FSR 571. High clearance and 4WD are recommended from here. It is 14.0 miles to the Kennebec Pass Trailhead from US 160.

Route

Kennebec Pass Trailhead, elevation 11,600 feet, is located at the head of La Plata Canyon and near the northern terminus of the La Plata range. The Colorado Trail passes through the parking lot.

Conscientious trail builders recommend an excess of caution on the quite solid trail.

Begin by walking west on an unusually level and languid segment of the cross-state trail. Midsummer, corn husk lily, little sunflower, delphinium and osha are tall bloomers. American bistort, rosy paintbrush, and Coulter's daisy are bountiful.

At 1.2 miles, leave the Colorado Trail and take the left branch onto the Sharkstooth Trail at a well-signed junction. Frequently visited Taylor Lake is just a few steps further.

Walking south, the mountains in the western La Platas provide an everevolving vista. At 2.0 miles, the trail switchbacks and starts uphill while swinging west around the base of the southern terminus of Indian Trail Ridge.

The Sharkstooth Trail is a testament to the heyday of trail building. Beside the trail is a hand-carved sign, "Warning Unstable Rock." The remarkable footpath maintains a dirt surface as it threads through a substantial talus field. Listen and watch for pikas. Whipple's penstemon and fireweed grow in stone cracks.

The treadway makes a rising traverse up a flowery hillside to surmount "Bear Creek Pass" at 2.5 miles, elevation 11,920 feet. It is on the divide between La Plata Canyon and Bear Creek Basin. Directly across to the west is

Sharkstooth Pass, a mere 16 feet higher. To its right is the trail's namesake peak. The La Sal Mountains and Lone Cone are visible in the northwest.

The view of Sharkstooth and Centennial peaks gives pause at Bear Creek Pass.

If the full trek seems too daunting, before turning around, consider tacking on Point 12,117'. It is less than 0.2 mile south of the pass with 200 feet of climbing. A social trail transitions to a stable talus field. You will be rewarded with an incomparable view of Bear Creek Basin and a ring of summits.

To continue on to Sharkstooth Pass, switchback into the basin on an impeccable dirt track with stones piled up on either side. At the base of the talus passage, the trail turns southwest descending to 11,000 feet.

In spite of all the markers, it is easy to lose sight of the path in Bear Creek Basin. When it disappears, scrounge around for it in the foliage. Over-sized blazes grew up with Engelmann spruce. Walk from blaze to blaze and watch for occasional rockpile cairns.

In wet years, the basin is flush with water. Expect to get your feet wet crossing 17 small streams and sloshing through spongy bogs. Cascades tumble over walls. Thirsty deep purple monkshood grow beside brooks. Pass left of two tarns on your watery way.

Above: Centennial Peak rises in the distance above a meticulously engineered talus passage.

Right: Wildflowers and water fill every crack in upper Bear Creek Basin.

The path takes direct aim at Centennial Peak and initiates an uphill grade at 4.2 miles. It crosses a burbling stream hidden under rock and elegantly negotiates talus run-out zones.

The Historic Highline Loop branches right onto the Bear Creek Trail at 4.6 miles. For information on the full loop, please see Indian Trail Ridge. A population of hallucinogenic amanita mushrooms lives at this junction. Let their white-spotted, brilliant red coloring serve as a warning.

A clear view of the pass opens at 5.2 miles. Plow through another block field on masterfully laid stones fit for a patio. The treadway zigs and zags to get above a minor cliff band. In August, Arctic and bottle gentian bloom beside the path.

The headwall climb initiates at 11,450 feet. Switchbacks mitigate the incline, the path is ultra-smooth, and climbing relaxed. Crowding the passage is an entire hillside of dazzling mixed bouquets featuring columbine.

Arrive on Sharkstooth Pass after 6.2 miles and 1,500 feet of vertical. A weathered sign lists the official elevation as 11,936 feet. Passes always reveal

The photograph above shows hikers on a trail.

Hikers climb the final switchback below Sharkstooth Pass and the daunting peak. a whole new world and, indeed, Hesperus Mountain captivates through the westward window. The banded peak marks the northern boundary of the traditional homeland of the Navajo, eternally bridging this place with the past. The Abajo Mountains are visible in the western reaches.

Centennial Peak and Sharkstooth Peak tempt from the saddle but they are not generally climbed from this approach. They are covered elsewhere in this guide.

If the weather is not threatening, saunter back while watching for marmots scampering in talus piles and deer foraging in the woods. Large herds of elk tend to congregate in upper Bear Creek Basin.

In autumn, Arctic gentian plays the ghost of summer past.

BURRO MOUNTAIN, 11,580'

You are always nearer the divine and the true sources of power than you think. The lure of the distant and the difficult is deceptive. The great opportunity is where you are.

— John Burroughs

Burro Mountain is a stand-alone summit west of the principal range. It is the most northerly ranked peak in the La Plata Mountains. The Burro Benchmark affords a keen lookout west to Sleeping Ute, north to Lone Cone, east to Indian Trail Ridge, and south to Hesperus Mountain. Burro is perhaps the most humble prominence in the range and one of the very few easily claimed La Plata crests. A walk in the woods leads to a ramble across the linear northern edge. Return as you came or take one of two loops back to Windy Gap.

ABOUT THIS HIKE
Distance: Out-and-back to Burro Benchmark, 3.2 miles; South Loop, 3.7 miles; North Loop, 5.0 miles
Elevation Gain: Burro Benchmark, 600 feet; South Loop, 850 feet; North Loop, 1,050 feet
Time: 2:00 to 3:30
Route Surface: off-trail and Forest Service roads
Class: 2
Exposure: none
Navigation: moderate

Travel

Begin measuring distance at the US 160 and CO 184 intersection in Mancos. In a 4WD vehicle with decent clearance, travel north on CO 184 toward Dolores. In 0.3 mile, at the sign for Mancos State Park, turn right on Montezuma CR 42. See the west side of the La Platas from a fresh perspective as you pass by scattered ranches. At 5.5 miles, the road becomes FSR 561, West Mancos Road. Pass the Transfer Campground at 10.3 miles where pavement ends. Stay on FSR 561 at 11.1 miles. Pass the Aspen Guard Station at 11.9 miles. Roll through a mature aspen and ponderosa forest and turn right at mile 12.4 on FSR 350, Spruce Mill Road. (FSR 561 becomes the Aspen Loop Trail which goes to Windy Gap but it takes considerably longer.) At 18.9

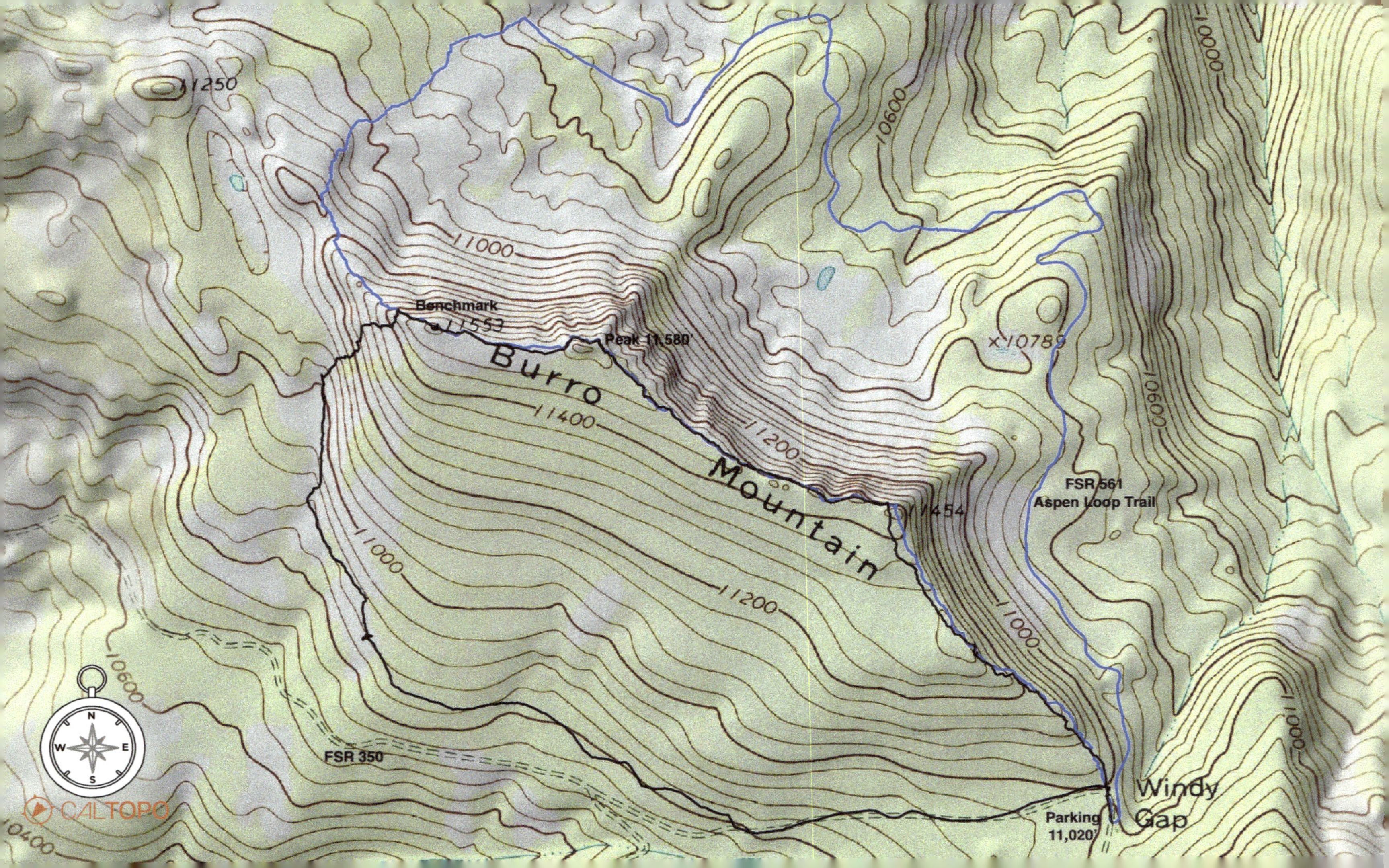

CALTOPO
11250
11000
10600
10000
Benchmark 11,553
Peak 11,580'
x 10789
Burro Mountain
11400
11200
11200
11,454
FSR 561 Aspen Loop Trail
11000
10600
11000
10000
10600
10400
FSR 350
Parking 11,020'
Windy Gap

miles, the FSR 346 spur to the Twin Lakes and Sharkstooth trailheads turns off to the right. Stay straight on rocky and rutted FSR 350. Park at Windy Gap, 19.8 miles from US 160.

Route

Forest Service Road 350 and FSR 561, the Aspen Loop Trail, meet in Windy Gap, elevation 11,020 feet. The South Loop returns to Windy Gap on FSR 350 and the North Loop returns on FSR 561. To begin the hike, walk a few steps back on FSR 350 and then ascend northwest on Burro Mountain's southeast ridge. There is no trail but it is easy to weave through the timber and climb over fallen logs. The forest floor is blanketed with myrtle blueberry.

By 0.2 mile, you will be walking along the north drop. From Point 11,454' at 0.7 mile, there is a big-swing view to all points north. Skimming the horizon are Lone Cone, the San Miguel Mountains, Lizard Head, and the Wilson fourteeners. At mid-range is Indian Trail Ridge. The Bear Creek drainage is in the trench. In the foreground, FSR 561 weaves through stands of conifer burned in the Burro Fire of 2018.

Walk along the pleasant northern rim toward the summit of Burro Mountain. The mountain

The first wide-open views from the ridge provide a welcome spot to take a break.

Left: An unusual benchmark-on-a-pole was placed in 1958.

Below: Lovely heartleaf arnica is abundant in the mountain's forests.

splintered and shed to form the rock glacier on the north slope. Small stone plates clink underfoot.

Stand on the high point of Burro Mountain at 1.3 miles. Peak 11,580' is not labeled on the La Plata topographical map but there is a peak register on the summit. From this relatively lofty vantage point locate Engineer Mountain and look into the Weminuche Wilderness. The Burro Benchmark is a short distance further and worth the 0.3 mile jaunt.

The benchmark was placed on Point 11,553' by the Department of Agriculture in 1958. It rests on a small shattered-rock crest with the mountain's only circular panorama. Burro's raw-boned and snow-clad

West Block neighbors are south: Sharkstooth and Centennial peaks, Lavender Peak, Hesperus Mountain, and Helmet Peak. Retrace your steps for the easiest route back. Otherwise, try one of these options.

South Loop

Walk down the northwest ridge for 0.1 mile. Drop 400 feet southwest down a very steep slope taking aim off Sleeping Ute Mountain.

As the pitch levels out, walk south and then southeast along the base of the mountain making the most of open avenues through the conifer. Turn east upon reaching FSR 350 at approximately 3.1 miles, 10,800 feet. The road ascends gradually back to Windy Gap.

Aiming for the nearest clump of trees in this photo will minimize the tedious talus-walking descent of the north face.

North Loop

The North Loop is the most demanding and rewarding of the three choices. Traversing Class 2+ block fields can be slow going but the rock glacier affords a wide open vista.

From the benchmark, pick your way down the rock glacier on the northwest ridge. Much of the rock is on the move and wobbles underfoot.

Cross a saddle at 1.9 miles, elevation 11,180 feet, and begin looking for a good line across the talus field to the northeast. If you grow weary of rock

hopping, walk among the trees edging the glacier. Mid-summer, heart leaf arnica grows in the shade of the forest.

Navigation is not critical. Walk north or east and you will intersect FSR 561, the Aspen Loop Trail, at about 2.4 miles, elevation 10,760 feet. The 4WD track rolls through a pretty forest. There's a good chance it will be free of vehicles. The burn was scattered in the Burro Fire zone and many trees were left unscathed. All along are fabulous views of the north face and summit of Burro Mountain. The road descends to 10,600 feet and then rises gently back to the starting point.

CUMBERLAND MOUNTAIN, 12,388'

Trees are the earth's endless effort to speak to the listening heaven.
— Rabindranath Tagore

Cumberland Mountain is accessible and friendly for hikers of all abilities. The stem-and-loop takes in an old-growth Engelmann spruce forest and a spectrum of superb wildflowers along the Colorado Trail. Visit the spectacularly perched Muldoon Mine ruins and then climb off-trail up the welcoming east ridge. While the peak is a speedy climb from the Kennebec Pass Trailhead this route from the east offers greater biodiversity and two-wheel drive vehicle access.

ABOUT THIS HIKE

Distance: 5.2 miles
Elevation Gain: 2,200 feet
Time: 3:30 to 5:00
Route Surface: Colorado Trail, off-trail
Class: 2
Exposure: none
Navigation: easy
Additional Map: Monument Hill, Colorado 7.5' USGS Quad

Travel

Measure distance from Main Avenue and 25th Street in Durango. Driving west, 25th Street transitions to Junction Creek Road and then to La Plata CR 204. Stay straight at 2.9 miles as CR 205 goes off to the right, following a sign for the Colorado Trail. At 3.5 miles pavement turns to dirt and the road becomes FSR 171. Pass the Junction Creek Campground at 4.9 miles. Wind up the broad gravel road with some washboard. Pass the Animas Overlook (last facilities) at 10.6 miles and continue along the western flank of Barnes Mountain. The road narrows and grows increasingly rocky. It is never steep so 2WD vehicles with good clearance and sturdy tires should reach the trailhead. At 14 miles the road gets really rough (sharp rocks!) and becomes a shelf with aspen protecting the huge drop. The view of Silver and Lewis mountains is superlative. Stay on the main road as tracks branch. At 15.4

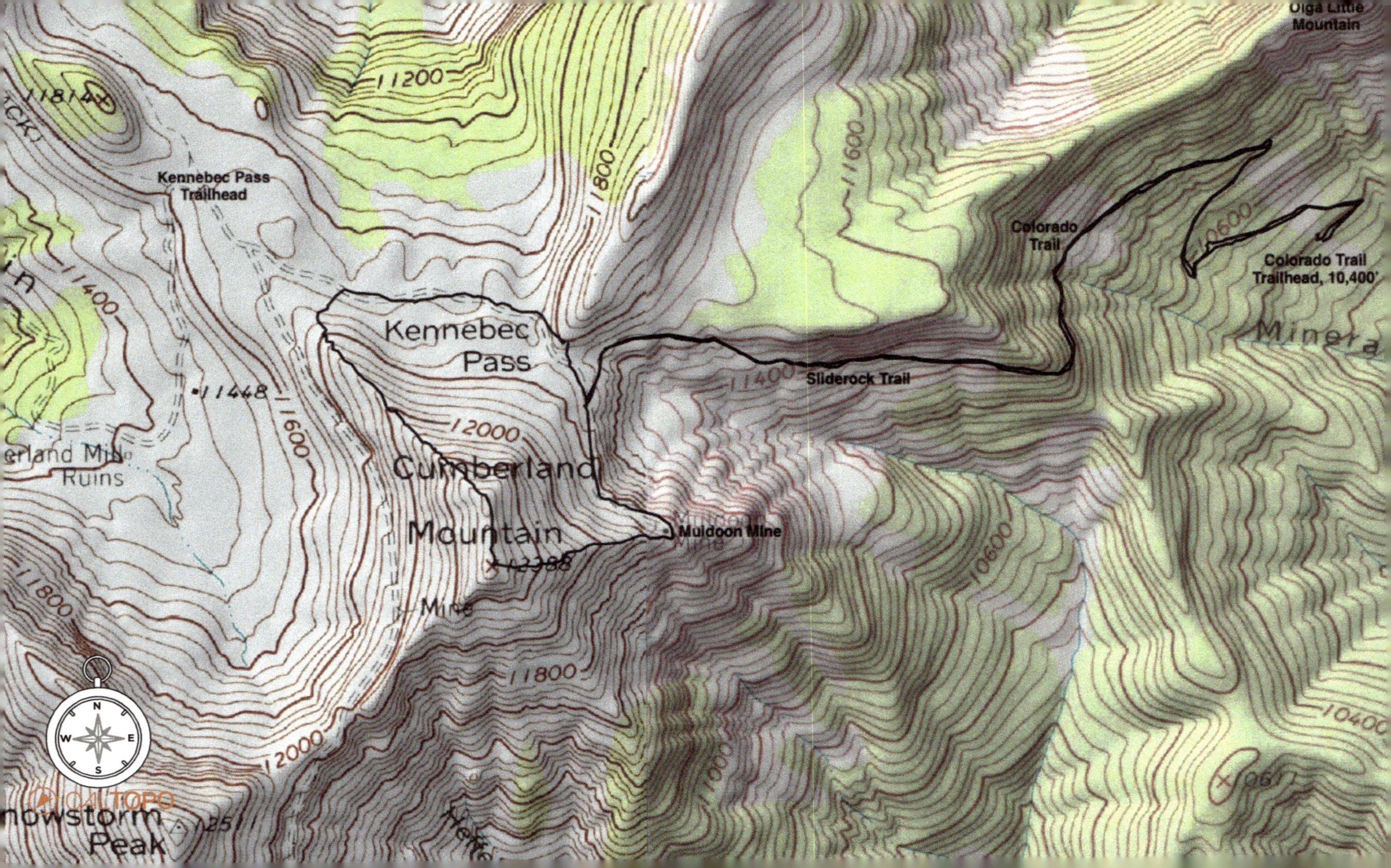

Olga Little Mountain
Kennebec Pass Trailhead
Kennebec Pass
Cumberland Mountain
Mine
Muldoon Mine
Sliderock Trail
Colorado Trail
Colorado Trail Trailhead, 10,400'
Minera
erland Mine Ruins
N W S E
CALTOPO
Snowstorm Peak
11200
11800
11600
11400
11600
10600
11400
11448
12000
11800
12000
10600
10400
N W S E

miles, go through a little pass to the north side of the ridge. A wild view of the San Juan Mountains opens at 19.2 miles. At 20.9 miles the road splits. Go left, following the sign for the Colorado Trail on FSR 171N. The road narrows and gets even rockier. Watch for a small sign for the Colorado Trail on the right side of the road at 21.5 miles. There is plenty of good parking.

Route

Begin on the north side of the road. On an excellent path rising from the trailhead at elevation 10,400 feet, allow yourself to be wound up and around on gentle switchbacks through deep woodsy glades and luscious wildflowers. In consort with receding snow are a bounty of glacier lily, spring beauty, mule's ears, and red columbine.

Groves of old-growth Engelmann spruce are the finest anywhere in the region. They are the deepest forest green with pale and delicate new needles. The oldest known living spruce in Colorado is more than 850 years old. Trees with trunks three feet in diameter are about 500 years of age. There is a group of four giants 0.8 mile up the trail rising to 200 feet. A common growth pattern creates a curve at the base of the tree. Their swooped trunks are surely four feet thick. Living in their shade on the forest floor are Jacob's ladder, white and purple violet, and strawberry.

At 1.2 miles, emerge from the trees. Here, the Colorado Trail shares the trackway with the aptly named Sliderock Trail. The trail platform is thin and marginal, prone to obliteration by scree slides and rocks peeling off the carmine columnar cliffs directly above. It is suitable for hikers but duly respected by local mountain bikers, most of whom resort to hike-a-bike. The climbing route up the east ridge of Cumberland is now in full view.

At 1.8 miles, 11,740 feet, a post marks the junction with the Muldoon Mine trail. Turn south and travel on the historic mining track beneath the east face of Cumberland Mountain.

After big winters, a snow sheet tends to linger in a gully between the junction and the mine. Crossing can be treacherous. The safest option is usually to drop below the snow before regaining the track.

The Muldoon Mine is perched on an east-facing terrace dug into the mountain. The mining claim was patented in the early 1880s but there is no record of production prior to 1917. It was worked for gold and silver for two years and again from 1935 until 1936 by early settler Herman Dalla.

The porch of the living quarters takes advantage of the drop-away view. The railroad track is interspersed with divinely fragrant phlox where it

Left: Even before being tilted by time, this seems a pretty dangerous way to do some ordinary business.

Below: Emerging from the trees on the Sliderock Trail, the destination appears clearly directly ahead.

clings to the precipitous edge. A bright yellow generator sits just inside the door of the workshop. A two seater outhouse is listing precariously over oblivion.

Left: Centuries-old mature Engelmann spruce display their impressive height and characteristic swoop at the trunk's base.

From the mine, climb the broad grassy ridge to the summit, a 570-foot ascent. The ridge pitches up toward the crest but foot platforms are good. The incline yields startling and revealing views of Lewis Mountain. What appears to be a broad, hulking eminence when seen from Durango, is

actually a curved ridge which is narrow and exposed for three miles.

Crest the peak at 2.4 miles. Cumberland Mountain has a talus summit with a large bivouac for wind protection. The panorama from the top affords an unmatched perspective on the West Block of the La Platas. Distant peaks in the San Juans look like a choppy sea.

Alpine flowers are flung all over the crest. All summer long you will see dotted and snowball saxifrage, fairy candelabra, mouse-ear chickweed, sky pilot, old man of the mountain, purple fringe, alpine avens, and deep rooted spring beauty.

To create a loop in the alpine, descend the northwest ridge on a social trail trampled into scree and dirt. Our route hooks back shy of the Kennebec Pass Trailhead but it would be a simple diversion to walk there.

For that matter, the easiest climb up Cumberland is from the terminus of the La Plata Canyon Road. It is less than one mile and 770 feet of elevation gain from Kennebec Pass to the peak.

As the ridge dissipates, simply cut north to rejoin the Colorado Trail. Turn east and stroll 0.3 mile to Kennebec Pass. Living in the moist swale are marsh marigold, elephant head, Parry's primrose, king's and queen's crown, a variety of paintbrush, and fringed gentian.

At 11,740 feet, the pass is the low point between Cumberland Mountain and Kennebec Peak. If you'd like to take in a second mountain, Kennebec is only 0.7 mile north with 370 feet of elevation gain. Close the loop at the trail to Muldoon Mine. It is a fast trek back to the trailhead.

Descending toward the Kennebec Pass Trailhead makes for a pleasant alternative to retracing your steps.

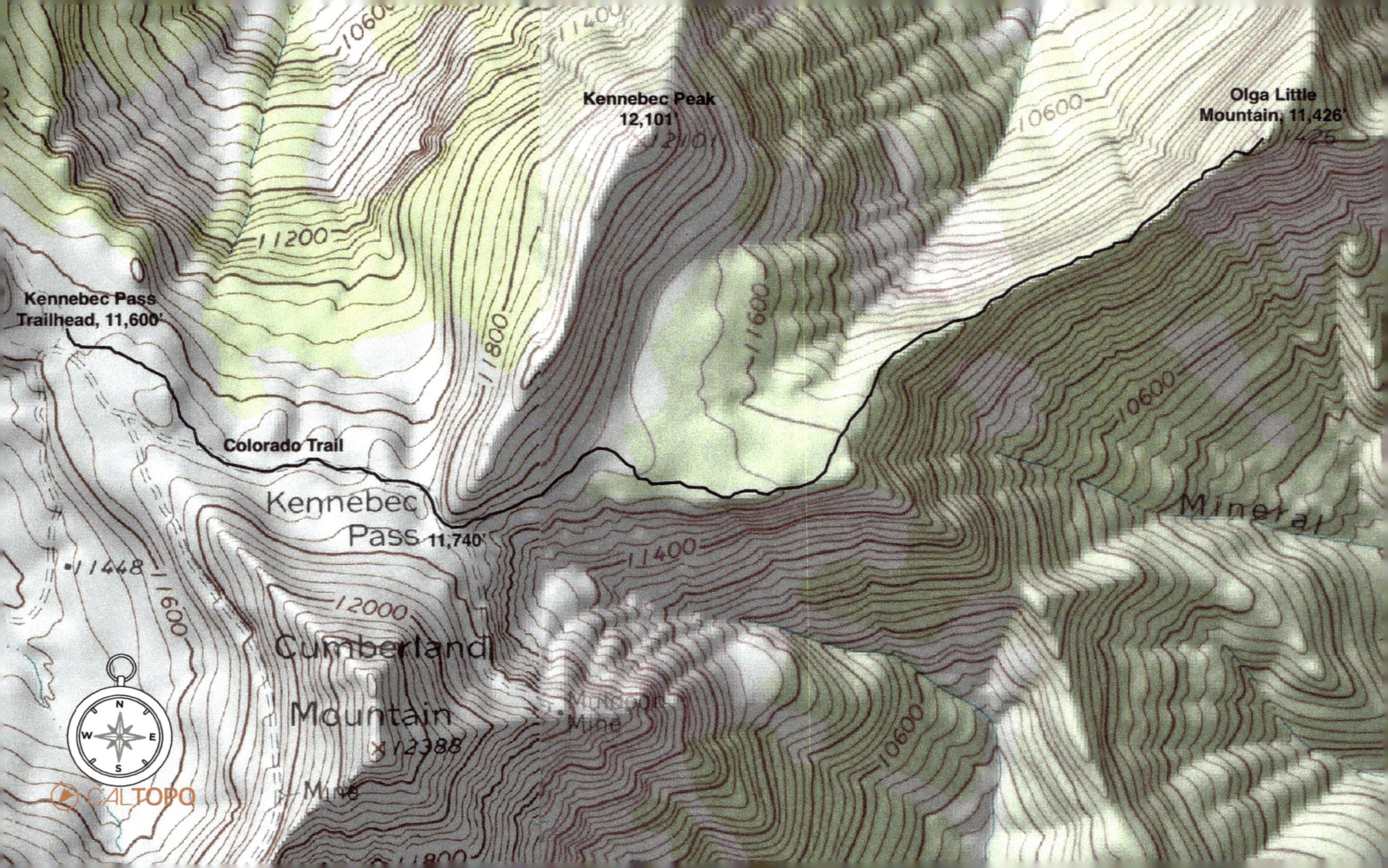

Kennebec Peak
12,101'
Olga Little
Mountain, 11,426'
11200
10600
10600
Kennebec Pass
Trailhead, 11,600'
11800
11600
Colorado Trail
Kennebec
Pass 11,740'
Mineral
11,448
11,600
11400
12000
Cumberland
Mountain
x 12388
Mine
10600
10600
11800
N W S E
CALTOPO

OLGA LITTLE MOUNTAIN, 11,426'

To you, Olga Little of Hesperus, Colorado!
Wherever mining men gather, and wherever tales are told
of the days of gold and silver in this great State of Colorado, a part of
that glory will always land upon your name.

— Ralph Edwards
"This is Your Life" TV show, 1958

Olga Little Mountain, with only 146 feet of prominence, is noteworthy for its historical significance. The diminutive crest was named and designated in 1983 for Olga Little (1885-1970), a German immigrant, who lived on a ranch in Mayday with her husband. From 1909 to 1949 she was a packer, using her string of burros to carry in supplies to men working at all of the La Plata mines. While Olga regularly hauled out ore, she once saved 18 starving men by having them hang onto her burros' tails while walking through a blizzard to safety. The mountain is more troublesome to visit than many higher peaks. Willow bashing and plowing through snarled trees is unavoidable. Wear jeans, your burro-riding boots, and cowboy up.

ABOUT THIS HIKE
Distance: 4.2 miles
Elevation Gain: 850 feet
Time: 3:00 to 4:00
Route Surface: Colorado Trail, primarily off-trail, thick willow stands and brush
Class: 2+
Exposure: mild
Navigation: moderate

Travel

Measure distance from the junction of US 160 and La Plata Canyon Road, CR 124. After passing the hamlet of Mayday the road turns to smooth dirt at 4.6 miles. In 8.5 miles the roadbed deteriorates with sharp, sizable rocks. At 12.0 miles the road splits; take the left track, FSR 571. High clearance and 4WD are recommended from here. It is 14.0 miles to the Kennebec Pass Trailhead from US 160.

Olga Little Mountain (right) and the complete route from the Colorado trail are revealed in this photo taken from Cumberland Mountain.

Route

The Colorado Trail goes right through the parking lot at the Kennebec Pass Trailhead, elevation 11,600 feet. Walk east toward Kennebec Pass through a moist landscape lush with willows and wildflowers. Water pulses from springs beside the trail and threads its way through an alpine marsh located high on an east-west running divide separating the headwaters of the La Plata River and the South Fork of Hermosa Creek.

Kennebec Pass, elevation 11,740 feet, is in the squeeze between Cumberland Mountain and Kennebec Peak. Just before topping the pass at 0.7 mile look for a thin little track flanking the southwest slope of Kennebec Peak about 100 feet above the Colorado Trail. The social trail is a welcome assist across the steep hillside. Look to the northeast and search out Olga Little Mountain 300 feet *below* your perch!

Its job done, the wildcat trail disappears on a broad platform in corn husk lily heaven. Take stock of your location and consider your plan for reaching the southwest ridge of Olga Little Mountain. While the ridge is only 0.6 mile from here, stands of willows make the going tough and the way obscure.

We have tried many alternate routes. The best is the most direct. Begin by walking east just below the willow line and above a red earth slope. Then barge into the willows holding an eastward bearing. Follow paths of least vegetative resistance; scraggly trees are some help. Swing with the platform as it curves northeast and necks down onto the south- west ridge.

Open rock and views of your goal punctuate the mostly forested ridge out to the summit.

The narrow, willow-free spur running out to Olga Little Mountain begins at 11,520 feet and extends another 0.6 mile. The ridge has a wild feel and will challenge most hikers. I like to picture Olga, small but mighty, dodging trees and balancing confidently on chopped gray rocks.

Descend for 0.4 mile to a saddle at 11,280 feet. Watch your footing and

The trees part suddenly, revealing the elongated and surprisingly open top of the mountain. stay right on the thin crest. If you must bypass an obstacle, return immediately to the razorback. The trees were trimmed since I first visited this peak and I expect elk hunters are to thank for enhancing the passage. Judging from all the scat, elk are plentiful. There are occasional views of the peak. Climb down through brick-colored blocks in the Cutler Formation. If your timing is good, blooming red columbine complements the rock. Once you

Late in life, in 1963, Olga poses with her longtime companion and favorite burro "Mutt."

Used by permission of the Animas Museum, Durango, CO

bottom out, there is only 0.2 mile remaining with 146 feet of vertical. It is best to track along a few feet off the spine on the north side. Climb the summit blocks from the north as well.

Top out on the linear summit at 2.1 miles. Judging from the peak register, only a couple of parties each year visit the red mountain and they are either elk hunting or paying homage to Colorado's only female jack packer. Look out over the familiar La Plata lineup and then circle around to see the San Miguel Mountains, Grenadier Range, and Needle Mountains. (Standing on the rim at Fort Lewis College there's a straight visual up Junction Creek to Olga Little Mountain.) Now you may reverse your gaze and see Durango to the southwest.

Olga Little Mountain from Kennebec Peak

The two mountains pair well. Climb Kennebec Peak and then walk a few paces back before initiating a grassy plunge southeast to the platform at roughly 11,640 feet. Walk east to intersect Olga's southwest ridge. Willow bashing is unavoidable.

CALTOPO
Parking Platform
10,960'
Helmet Peak
Saddle 11,560'
Echo Creek
River
Mine
Gibbs Peak
Prospect
Bench
Rush Basin
Mine
TRAIL
L A   P L A T A
Blacker Peak
Snively Peak

HELMET PEAK, 11,969'
TO RUSH BASIN

There is a way that nature speaks, that land speaks.
Most of the time we are simply not patient enough,
quiet enough to pay attention to the story.

— Linda Hogan

Small in stature with a sun-drenched south ridge approach, Helmet Peak is ready to climb early in the season. Just one mile and one thousand feet of ascent lands you on the summit. Situated west of the principle range, the stand-alone mountain provides a unique perspective on west-facing walls. Helmet is the launch point for a two-and-a-half mile ridgeline traverse to Rush Basin, a hidden, high alpine cirque.

ABOUT THIS HIKE
Distance: Round trip to Helmet Peak, 2.0 miles;
          Round trip to Rush Basin, 6.8 miles
Elevation Gain: Helmet Peak, 1,020 feet; Rush Basin, 2,770 feet
Time: Helmet Peak, 2:00 to 3:00; Rush Basin, 4:30 to 5:30
Route Surface: off-trail, some talus, light scrambling on ridge to Rush Basin
Class: 2, 2+ to Rush Basin
Exposure: none
Navigation: moderate
Additional Map: Rampart Hills, Colorado 7.5' USGS Quad

Travel

From the US 550/160 intersection in Durango, travel west on US 160 for 24.7 miles to the signed Echo Basin Road and turn right on Montezuma CR 44. Measure distance from here. Stay on the main road, passing old homesteads and hay meadows. In 2.4 miles pavement turns to gravel and the road transitions to FSR 566. The roadbed deteriorates at 3.8 miles where winter plowing stops. The track climbs steadily through scrub oak to a cattle guard at 6.4 miles. Directly east is The Hogback. At 6.8 miles take the right fork, staying on FSR 566. At 8.0 miles the road forks again; turn right. 4WD with high clearance and sturdy tires are needed on the choppy track. Turn right on FSR 322 at 10.3 miles and cross a talus field at 11 miles. Go over a little pass, elevation 10,951 feet, between The Hogback and Helmet Peak. Park on the rocky parking platform at 11.5 miles.

Route

There are multiple routes up the mountain; this one is direct and safe. It begins just south of the pass between The Hogback and Helmet Peak. The mountain lies due east but rock glaciers and spectacular cliffs prohibit a direct approach. Just beyond the parking platform at elevation 10,960 feet, the road does a triple split. Take the leftmost branch through a talus field.

In 0.1 mile leave the road and launch east-southeast up a slope with a consistent pitch. Follow the glades in the spruce-fir forest, keeping the prominent rock glacier rolling off the summit ridge on your left. There is a maze of roadways on the slope and you will cross abandoned tracks several times. Reach the treed saddle, elevation 11,580 feet, in 0.7 mile. There is a small opening revealing the West Block of the La Platas.

The summit is just 0.3 mile off with 400 feet of climbing remaining. Ascend the Class 2 south ridge, a mix of dirt and talus. A social trail comes and goes; just stay near the ridge top.

Crest Helmet Peak at one mile. From this westernmost lookout, regard

striated Hesperus Mountain, the towers of Lavender Peak, and steeply-pitched Spiller Peak presiding over Rush Basin. Lone Cone is a solitary thrust in the northwest; El Diente Peak, Mount Wilson, and Wilson Peak form a bulky cluster of fourteeners; and Lizard Head juts up radically.

Due west, the Helmet Peak rock glacier abuts The Hogback. The town of Mancos is 5,000 feet below on the valley floor. Point Lookout stands at the entrance of Mesa Verde National Park and to its right is Sleeping Ute Mountain. Unbounded views disappear into the blue distance as the Colorado Plateau extends south and west until it falls off the curve of the world.

Rush Basin Traverse

The optional ridge top traverse to Rush Basin adds 4.8 miles and 1,750 feet of climbing. Simply follow the ridge from Helmet to the northeast. Drop off the summit on a grassy slope, crossing an old wagon road. From the minor saddle at 11,420 feet climb and tag Point 11,490' at 1.5 miles.

Continue past Point 11,522', and go over the highest prominence of the hike, Point 12,201', at 3.1 miles.

The stark and colorful ridge is mostly unobstructed. There are a couple of easy scrambles on the spine and the 260-foot descent to the Spiller Peak saddle. Drop another 100 feet into the basin, reaching it at 3.4 miles, elevation 11,840 feet. In the center of the cirque sits a beautiful tundra-bound lake, headwaters of the East Mancos River.

To return, walk southwest on the irresistible and alluring bench, a tableland that rests between the out-going ridge and the river canyon well below. In about 0.9 mile, look for a wildcat trail leading from the bench to the ridge southwest of Point 12,201'. Retrace your steps over the top of Helmet Peak.

Cornices on the peak
often persist through
June, providing
additional
entertainment in a
unique setting.

ADVENTURERS

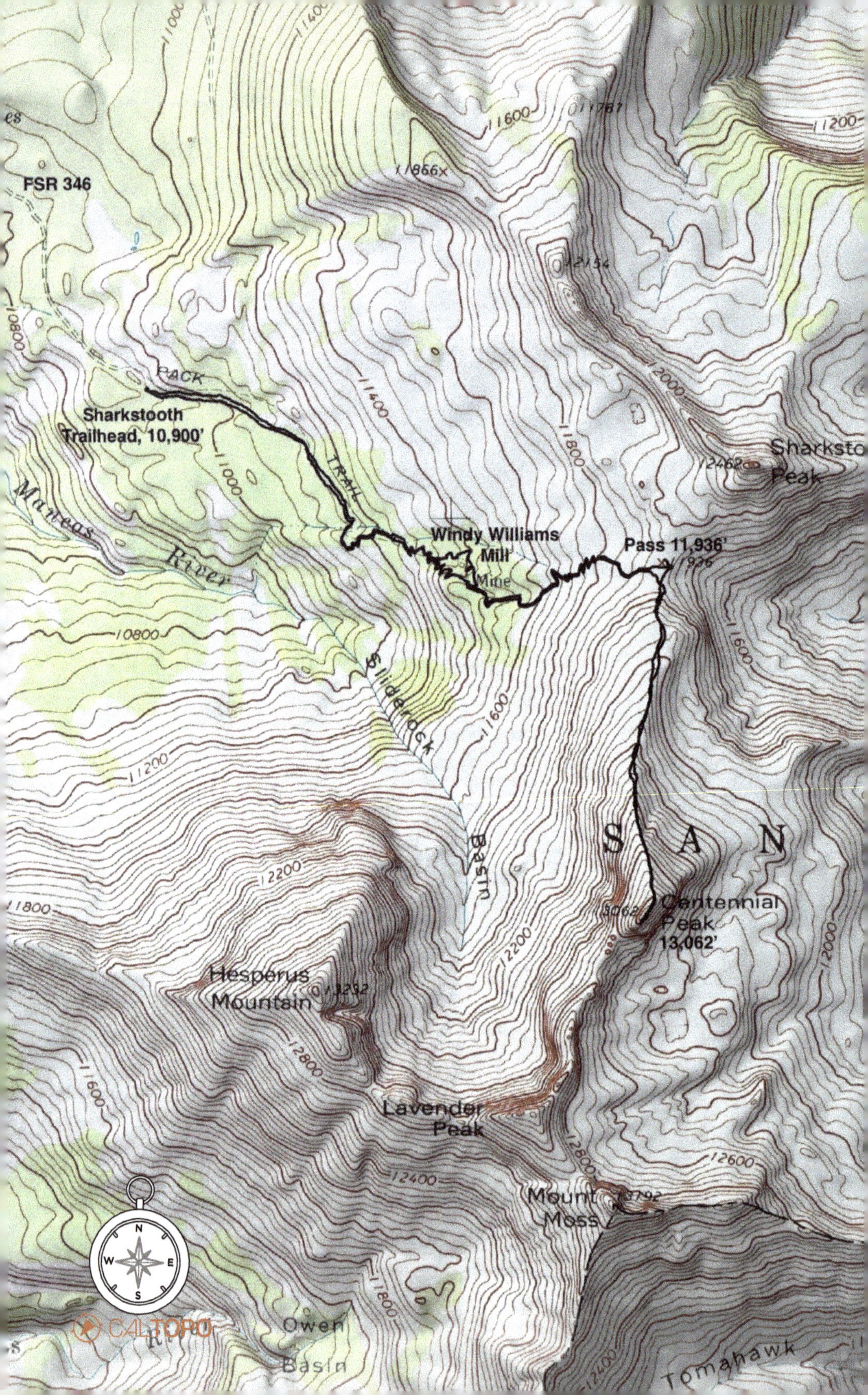

FSR 346
Sharkstooth
Trailhead, 10,900'
PACK
TRAIL
Maneas River
11000
10800
11200
11800
11600
11400
11000
11600
11800
11866x
12154
12462
Sharkstooth Peak
Windy Williams Mill
Mine
Pass 11,936'
11,936'
Sliderock Basin
11600
11600
S A N
12200
11200
12200
12200
11800
Hesperus Mountain
13292
Centennial Peak
13,062'
13062
12800
12400
12800
Lavender Peak
12600
11600
12600
Mount Moss
13792
N
W E
S
CALTOPO
11800
Owen Basin
12400
12400
Tomahawk

CENTENNIAL PEAK, 13,062'

I wish to speak a word for Nature,
for absolute freedom and wildness.

— Henry David Thoreau

Banded Mountain was renamed Centennial Peak in celebration of America's bicentennial in 1976. The mountain is an excellent first thirteener for teenagers. Mileage is short, elevation gain is moderate, and most of the climb is on-trail with light scrambling. The rugged face of the range is seen from the summit. Approach from the Sharkstooth Trail on the west side of the La Platas.

ABOUT THIS HIKE
Distance: 5.5 miles
Elevation Gain: 2,200 feet
Time: 3:00 to 5:00
Route Surface: trail, social trail, some talus
Class: 2+
Exposure: mild
Navigation: easy

Travel

Measure distance from the intersection of US 160 and CO 184 in Mancos. At the signal, turn north toward Dolores. In 0.3 mile, at the sign for Mancos State Park, turn right on Montezuma CR 42. At 5.5 miles, the road becomes FSR 561, West Mancos Road. Pass the Transfer Campground at 10.3 miles where pavement ends. Stay on FSR 561 at 11.1 miles. Pass the Aspen Guard Station at 11.9 miles. Roll through a mature aspen and ponderosa forest and turn right at mile 12.4 on FSR 350, Spruce Mill Road. It remains smooth and graded until mile 18.8. Turn on the right spur signed for the Twin Lakes and Sharkstooth trailheads, FSR 346. The next 1.5 miles require 4WD, good clearance, and sturdy tires. The track is rocky with potholes. There is dispersed camping along the road with ponds and a terrific view of Hesperus Mountain. Park in a small lot at the end of the road, 20.3 miles from US 160.

Route

The Sharkstooth Trail leaves from the east side of the parking lot at elevation 10,900 feet. On a well-established pathway enter an old growth forest. Look trailside for a particularly massive Colorado blue spruce. After you pass beneath the runout of the Sharkstooth rock glacier the age-old forest duff trail is spongy and soft. The canopy is atwitter with bird song. Mid-summer, brookcress and caraway crowd a tributary of the Mancos River. Head-high purple monks-hood contrast with delicate sprays of white osha.

In one mile, Hesperus Mountain, colorful and massive, is framed by deep green conifers. Hikers give little notice of switchbacks that lift them to sunny glades densely populated with bluebells and corn husk lilies.

In the alpine, reverie continues as the path plows through unimaginably lush gardens of hybridized Indian paintbrush, king's crown, columbine, and phlox.

Most alpinists will effortlessly cover the 1.8 miles to the Sharkstooth-Centennial saddle in an hour or less. Sizable cairns signal the final passageway to this unmistakable juncture. Here we leave the Sharkstooth Trail which proceeds east to join the Colorado Trail at Taylor Lake near Kennebec Pass.

The final talus march up from the saddle looks more challenging than it is.

The yellow dots scattered all over the tundra are the cheerful alpine sunflower, old man of the mountain. Warning: there is a generous sprinkling of elegant death camas. It has lance-like leaves and pretty pale white blossoms on foot-tall stems. One touch of the flower and then your tongue will make you sick. Eating this plant is potentially lethal for dogs.

From the pass, elevation 11,936 feet, Centennial Peak is 0.8 mile south with an additional 1,150 feet of climbing. It is straightforward and fun with intermittent stretches of social trail. Simply walk up the broad ridge, staying toward the east side.

Initially, walk up the tundra and locate a use trail that assists with a short, steep section. Clamber up a swath of large talus chunks. The grade

decreases at another expanse of tundra broken by patches of rock sheltering alpine sorrel.

The ridge narrows for the final 600 feet but there is little sense of exposure. If anything, it gets more playful. A worn path offers an off-ridge option to the west. It is helpful for bypassing an initial rock outcrop. Henceforth, scramblers may prefer to stay on the spine for the remainder of the summit ascent. There are a few sections where hands are helpful but it is all Class 2+ climbing on stable rock.

The higher you go the more outrageous the experience becomes. Light bounces off the columnar shafts and towers of imposing Lavender Peak. It is half a mile east of the horizontal bands pressed down by mighty Hesperus. The contrast is bedazzling.

Seen from afar, Centennial Peak has the same striping as Hesperus Mountain. Both are part of the La Plata Mountains laccolith. The peaks are composed of alternating layers of magma and banded hornfels, formed from the metamorphosis of sedimentary rock.

Reach 13,000 feet and blast up the red path to the summit. Whether or not this is your first thirteener, summit euphoria is guaranteed. From the garnet-colored crest the southern vista is unfathomably wild. Jutting from the peak is the ridge that experienced and bold climbers have traversed to Lavender. East of Lavender is Mount Moss.

The summit forms a proper point amongst its brethren high perches of the range.

Back in the forest on your return, divert onto a signed, short interpretive loop trail to see the historic Windy Williams Mill. Though minerals associated with gold were found here, the mine and boarding house were abandoned after only 115 days because valuable ore was scarce.

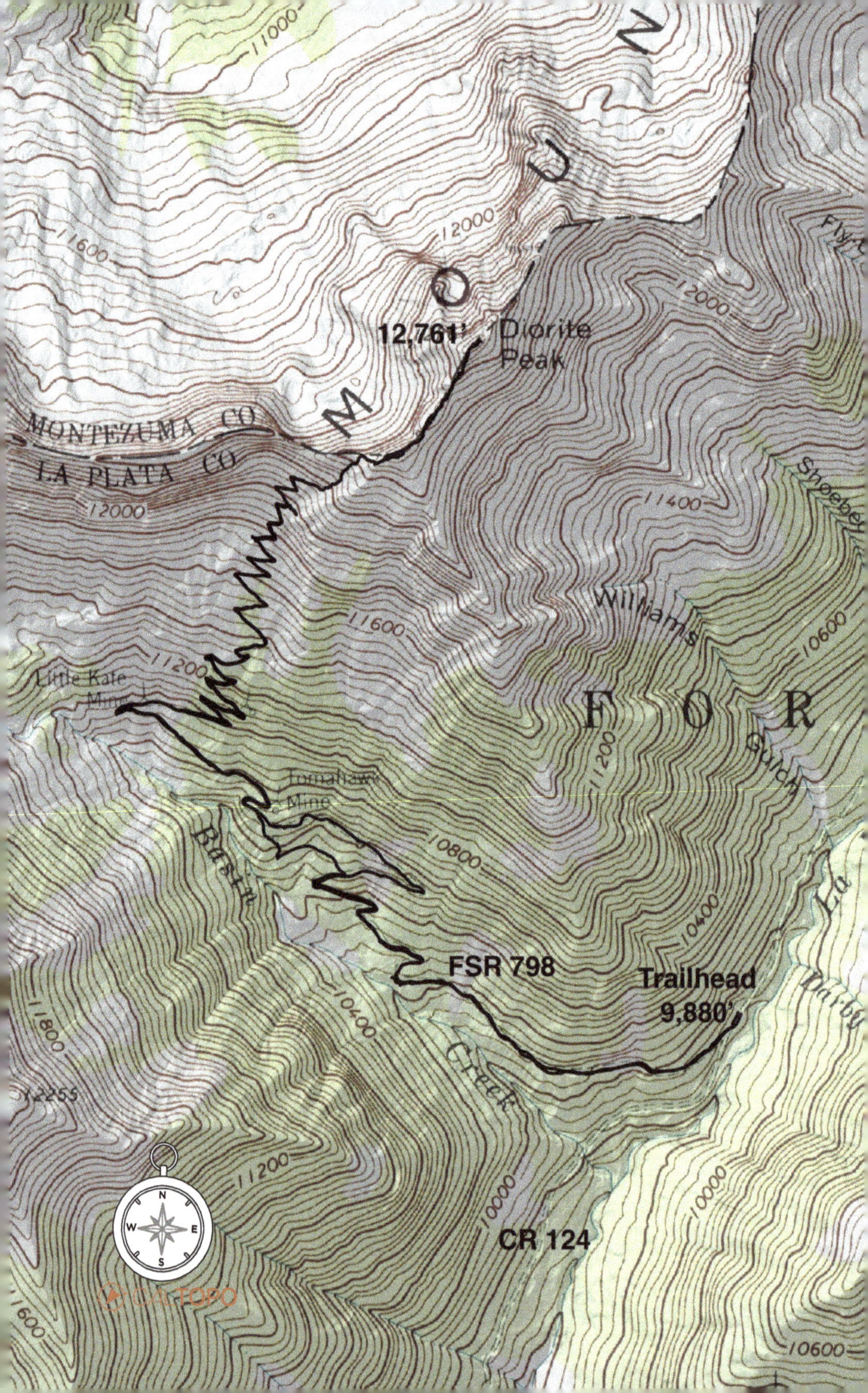
11000
11600
12000
12000
12,761' Diorite Peak
MONTEZUMA CO
LA PLATA CO
12000
11400
11600
Shoe...
11200
Williams Gulch
Little Kate Mine
F O R
10600
Tomahawk Mine
10800
11200
Basin
10400
FSR 798
Trailhead
9,880'
La Darby
Creek
10400
12255
10000
11200
11800
N
W E
S
10000
CR 124
11600
10600

DIORITE PEAK, 12,761'

Look at the flowers—for no reason.
It is simply unbelievable how happy flowers are.

— Osho

Diorite Peak is a skyscraper zenith, yet it is surprisingly welcoming and friendly. Anyone in solid shape can crest this mountain. The summit is accessed from the south so it may be climbed earlier in the summer than most peaks in the La Plata Range. For many locals, climbing Diorite in May is an annual rite of spring. Picturesque mining ruins begin just a mile up the trail.

ABOUT THIS HIKE
Distance: 7.6 miles
Elevation Gain: 3,000 feet
Time: 4:30 to 6:00
Route Surface: Forest Service Road, social trail, off-trail
Class: 2+
Exposure: moderate
Navigation: moderate

Travel

Measure distance from the junction of US 160 and La Plata Canyon Road, CR 124. After passing the hamlet of Mayday the road turns to smooth dirt at 4.6 miles. In 8.5 miles, the roadbed deteriorates with sharp, sizable rocks. A 2WD vehicle with good tires and moderate clearance should suffice. Park at 10.6 miles. The hike goes west up Forest Service Road 798 into Tomahawk Basin. There is room for a couple of vehicles on CR 124.

Route

From the parking pullout, elevation 9,880 feet, walk west up FSR 798, an historic wagon road. The aspen forest is occasionally interrupted with talus yards. Entrenched Basin Creek churns year-round.

Emerge from the woods in lower Tomahawk Basin. In 1.0 mile, the road splits at the Tomahawk shortcut trail. It punches up west of the tailings pile and Tomahawk stamp mill before rejoining the road. For a leisurely ascent, simply stay on the road by bearing right. Either way, you can admire the

Above: Now quiet, this stamp mill once filled the canyon with a deafening racket.

impressive mining ruins at close range.

The Tomahawk Mining Company built the stamp mill in 1904. Exploratory work was done on promising veins in the diorite stock. Recovery of precious metals was poor, at most 0.6 ounce of gold to the ton. Mining operations in Tomahawk Basin concluded in 1911. Incidentally, rockhounds have reported samples of precious amethyst in the upper basin.

The track makes a hairpin to the right at Little Kate Mine, 1.9 miles. Soon the ridge spanning Mount Moss and Diorite Peak is revealed to the north. Remain on the abandoned road as it switchbacks up the south-facing slope. The road fades and a social trail commences. After the rocky track, the green treadway is a relief, even if the grade steepens.

The trail passes close to beautifully crafted stone foundations. Wildflowers grow audaciously in the cracks. The path ends at a large mine cavern drilled into the side of the mountain. The next goal is the saddle, 300 vertical feet away. Simply climb north up the steep hillside to the minor divot in the ridge. Trekking poles are helpful for stair-stepping up flower platforms on renowned Columbine Hill.

Left: A hiking group covers the cliff-walled summit with little room to spare.

Mid-summer, the sheer numbers of columbine are staggering. These glorious yet gaudy flowers look like a product of a special effects studio. A dazzling assortment of wildflower bouquets compete with this state champion for all they are worth. Notable is Brandegee's clover, a study in velvet hot magenta.

This spot just below the saddle is known for its carpets of blue columbine in spring and summer.

From the saddle,12,300 feet, Mount Moss is two miles directly west. Resist the common urge to bridge this dangerous, impassible knife.

Diorite Peak is less than half a mile from the saddle. Turn east and climb on the ridge top, or just right of the rib on fragments of social trail.

The summit comes into view from a promontory. Descend to a shallow low point. The final 200 feet of climbing is Class 2+ on solid blocks of rock. The upper mountain is composed of the granitic diorite, an intrusive igneous rock dependable underfoot.

Approach the crest by means of a peninsular stone catwalk, experiencing the thrill of a narrow ridge with only a hint of the expected fright. A columnar cliff on the west face accentuates Diorite Peak's small crown at 3.8 miles. The peak falls off to the east less evenly but just as greatly. On a clear day, the vista of the San Juans is astounding.

In late spring, snow mixed with stony brilliance is visually captivating. Diorite resides as a stand-alone peak smack in the middle of the La Plata Range. On the West Block the alluring and intimidating Babcock trio is south and Mount Moss is due west. To its north are Lavender Peak, Hesperus Mountain, and Centennial Peak. Across La Plata Canyon is Kennebec Pass, and Cumberland, Lewis, and Silver mountains.

For the return, the simplest strategy is to walk back on your ascent route.

Lewis
Mountain
Little Ruby Gulch
La Plata
River
Ashland Gulch
Upper Parking
11,300'
Mine X
Eagle Pass
11,780'
Point 11,900'
Wallis Gulch
Mine Ruins
10,460'
Lewis Creek Road
Trailhead, 9,440'
CR 124
Fish Gulch
Point 11,391'
Saddle 11,020'
Puzzle Pass
MOUNTAIN
Baker
Peak
11,637'
Bald Knob
N
W E
S
CALTOPO

BALD KNOB, 11,637'

In the end, you won't remember the time you spent working in the office or mowing your lawn. Climb that goddamn mountain.

— Jack Kerouac

Visit historic mining structures while walking up Lewis Creek Road to Eagle Pass, the distinctive saddle between Lewis Mountain and Baker Peak. Give up 900 feet and then climb Bald Knob, the easternmost mountain in the La Platas. This strenuous climb to a peak relatively short in stature is almost entirely below timberline. However, the open, stand-alone summit affords an exclusive perspective on the range. Look out over Durango and afar into the Weminuche Wilderness.

ABOUT THIS HIKE

Distance: La Plata River, 11 miles; Mine Ruins, 7.4 miles; Upper parking, 4.8 miles
Elevation Gain: La Plata River 4,000 feet; Mine Ruins, 2,980 feet; Upper Parking, 2,140 feet
Time: 6:00 to 8:00 from the La Plata River
Route Surface: 4WD road, off-trail, social trail
Class: 2
Exposure: none
Navigation: challenging
Additional Map: Monument Hill, CO 7.5' USGS Quad

Travel

Measure distance from the junction of US 160 and La Plata Canyon Road, CR 124. After passing the hamlet of Mayday the road turns to smooth dirt at 4.6 miles. In 8.5 miles the roadbed deteriorates with sharp, sizable rocks. A 2WD vehicle with sturdy tires and moderate clearance may continue to Lewis Creek Road, CR 124A, at 9.4 miles. Turn right and park just before or after the bridge crossing the La Plata River. Vehicles with 4WD low, high clearance, and beefy tires may proceed up Lewis Creek Road. The serious track is steep and rocky for its entire length. Because the road abuts private land, parking is limited to the beginning of CR 124A at the La Plata River, the Gold King Mine ruins 1.8 miles up the road where the land owner has granted permission, and the upper parking platform at 3.1 miles on public land.

Route

Walking up Lewis Creek Road essentially doubles the overall effort but for most hikers it is unavoidable. Few vehicles are up to the demands of the steep and rock-laden track. Further, it is not uncommon for the road to be blocked by debris and a slidepath shortly before the Gold King Mine.

From the bridge across the La Plata River, elevation 9,440 feet, hike east up the chipped rock track. Please stay on the road, a public easement through private property. The walk is pleasant in an aspen forest with good flowers. Cross Ashland Gulch at 1.1 miles followed by the north fork of Lewis Creek.

Above: The parking area at the top of the road makes a sweet spot for a break.

Right: This miners' boarding house, long abandoned in the harsh environment, still bears witness to the skills of its builders.

Watch off the right side of the road for an historic boarding house associated with the Gold King Mine, 1.8 miles, 10,460 feet. The mine was located on the north bank of Lewis Creek. Large-scale production of gold and silver began in 1927 when La Plata Mines Company bought the property. Production was highest in 1937 then dwindled significantly until the mine ceased operations in 1943. The existing road and an aerial tramline connected the mine with the Gold King Mill on the La Plata River, two miles southwest. The mill was equipped with fifty, 1,000-pound stamps but seldom operated at more than one-third capacity. The mill was lost to fire in 2003.

The road splits at 3.0 miles. Take the left branch which passes by the upper parking platform at 11,300 feet. The road continues on but drivers are warned of a locked gate in half a mile. In late spring as snow recedes from the flat, glacier lilies are glowing little spots of pure yellow.

The road makes a right hairpin turn and ascends southeast. Go around

the gate, and anywhere in this vicinity leave the road and cut up to Eagle Pass. The pass, elevation 11,780 feet, is on a divide separating the waters of Lewis Creek from Junction Creek to the east. This is an alternative launch point for climbing Lewis Mountain.

Ascend south to Point 11,900'. Look past a weather station, radio transmitter, and other communication towers to the interlocking mountains west of La Plata Canyon.

The prominent knoll is the high point of the hike, standing taller even than Bald Knob. This is a good place to get your bearings. Bald Knob is the highest prominence nearby in the southeast. The hike stays on the ridge-crest over three rises and then descends to a saddle north of the peak. The first drop is pretty steep, one of several highly angled pitches. There is no trail on this fine little ridge with a mix of trees, shattered rock, and flowers. Watch for snowball saxifrage, kittentail, and purple fringe.

Point 11,391' is a crucial juncture and yet it is nondistinctive. Watch carefully for the ridge to split at 4.7 miles. Turn south and again, stay right on the spine, this time in a heavy conifer forest.

Drop to the saddle at 5.0 miles, 11,020 feet. A rudimentary hunter's trail makes shallow switchbacks up the steep north ridge.

Break out of the trees on the broad summit ridge at 11,620 feet. Walk west to the grassy, softly rounded crest, topping out at 5.5 miles. The peak is favored by hunters who sign the summit register year after year. One summer, orange sneezeweed on the mountaintop was covered in butterflies.

Bald Knob sits out in front of the La Plata range and the vantage point is spectacular. Southwest is Baker Peak and Silver Mountain. North is the span from Lewis Mountain to Olga Little Mountain. The disordered summits of the Weminuche Wilderness are on the eastern horizon.

Return to the saddle and search for a faint pathway heading northwest. It takes off slightly north of the saddle's low point. The trail begins by holding the contour and then it ascends easily and gradually. To stay on the subtle track, follow your trail intuition. It was maintained some time ago so look for cut logs as clues.

The thin treadway rises to tag the ridge east of Point 11,670'. It flanks the knoll on a contour and then climbs to meet the old road east of Point 11,900'. Stay on the two-track as it swings around the south side of the industrial knoll and proceeds beyond the locked gate.

The trees kindly withdraw along the linear summit ridge, providing surprisingly fine views.

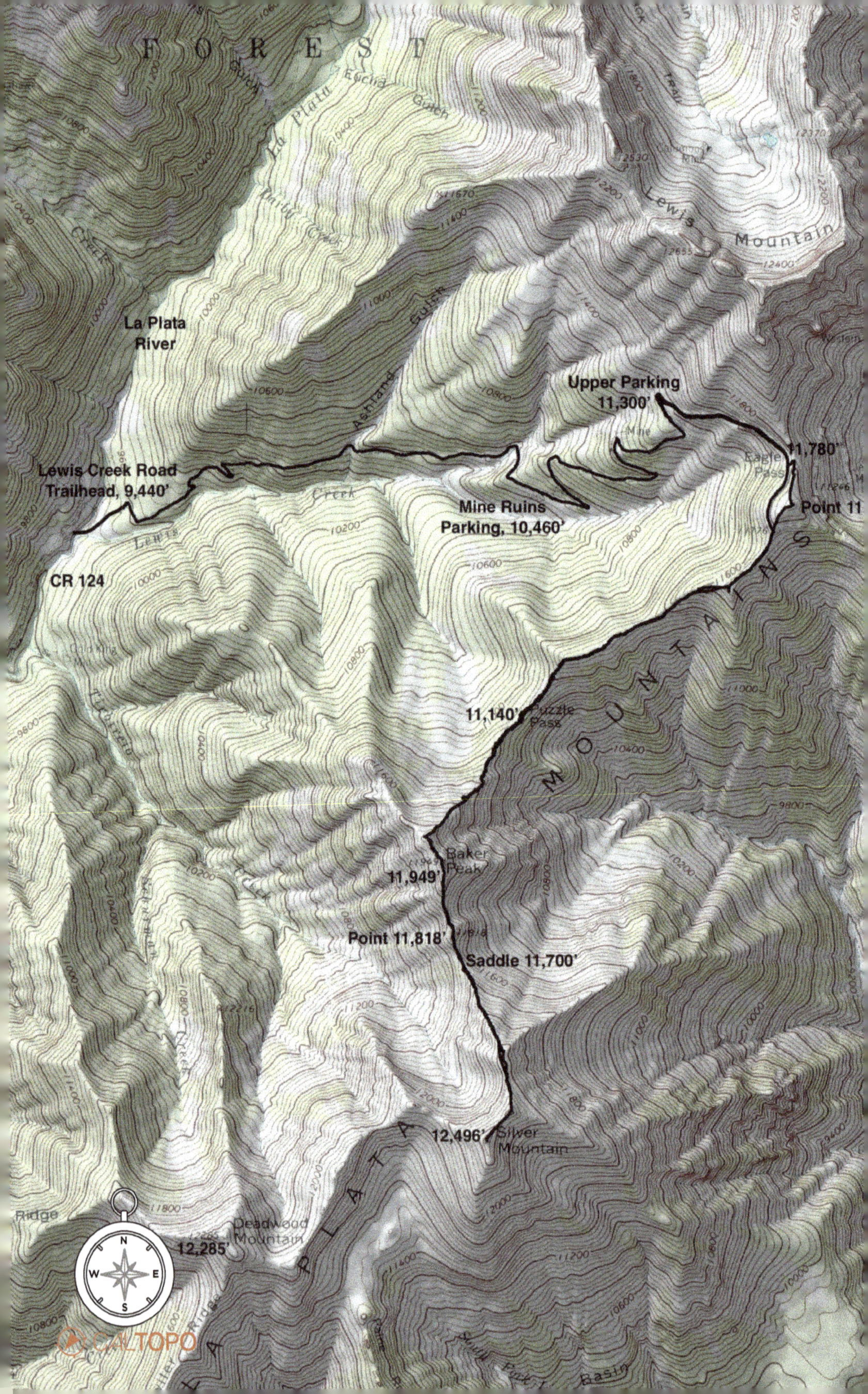

FOREST
La Plata
River
Lewis
Mountain
Upper Parking
11,300'
11,780'
Lewis Creek Road
Trailhead, 9,440'
Eagle
Pass
Point 11
Mine Ruins
Parking, 10,460'
CR 124
MOUNTAINS
11,140'
Puzzle
Pass
Baker
Peak
11,949'
Point 11,818'
Saddle 11,700'
12,496'
Silver
Mountain
Ridge
Deadwood
Mountain
12,285'
LA PLATA
N
W
E
S
CALTOPO

BAKER PEAK, 11,949'
TO SILVER MOUNTAIN, 12,496'

Returning to daily life after a trip to the mountains, I have often felt as though I were a stranger re-entering my country after years abroad, not yet adjusted to my return, and bearing experiences beyond speech.

— Robert Macfarlane

One of the charms of Baker Peak is that it doesn't make the playbook that ranked summits enjoy because there is only 249 feet of prominence from the Silver Mountain saddle. And yet, it is an extraordinary, multi-humped mountaintop lookout. The neglected summit is most often climbed by way of Silver Mountain. We are recommending an unconventional route that approaches from the north via Eagle Pass and curiously-named Puzzle Pass. Baker is a remote summit whether you walk or drive up the demanding Lewis Creek Road. The off-trail segment is multifaceted with steep slopes and ridges on good rock. The traverse to Silver Mountain cranks up the order of difficulty with increased effort and exposure.

ABOUT THIS HIKE
Distance to Baker Peak: La Plata River, 11.2 miles; Mine Ruins, 7.6 miles; Upper Parking, 5.0 miles
Distance to Silver Mountain: add 2.0 miles round trip
Elevation Gain to Baker Peak: La Plata River, 3,860 feet; Mine Ruins, 2,840 feet; Upper Parking, 2,000 feet
Elevation Gain to Silver Mountain: add 1,200 feet
Time: 6:00 to 8:00 from the La Plata River; add 1:30 to 2:30 for Silver Mountain
Route Surface: jeep track, off-trail, social trail
Class: 2+
Exposure: Baker Peak, mild; Silver Mountain, moderate
Navigation: moderate

Travel

Measure distance from the junction of US 160 and La Plata Canyon Road, CR 124. After passing the hamlet of Mayday the road turns to smooth dirt at 4.6 miles. In 8.5 miles the roadbed deteriorates with sharp, sizable rocks. A 2WD vehicle with sturdy tires and moderate clearance may continue to Lewis Creek Road, CR 124A, at 9.4 miles. Turn right and park just before or after the bridge crossing the La Plata River. Vehicles with 4WD low, high

clearance, and beefy tires may proceed up Lewis Creek Road. This serious track is steep and rocky for its entire length. Because the road abuts private land, parking is limited to the beginning of CR 124A at the La Plata River, the Gold King Mine ruins 1.8 miles up the road where the land owner has granted permission, and the upper parking platform at 3.1 miles on public land.

Route

Walking up Lewis Creek Road essentially doubles the overall effort but few vehicles are up to the demands of the steep and rock-laden track. From the bridge across the La Plata River, elevation 9,440 feet, hike east, climbing steadily. There are swatches of private land throughout the corridor. Please stay on the road, a public easement.

The road was cleaved into the south-facing slopes above Lewis Creek to serve the Gold King Mine at 1.8 miles, 10,460 feet. The picturesque, three story wooden building is one of the few remaining historic mining structures in the La Platas.

At 3.0 miles, branch left to access the upper parking platform at 11,300

feet. The road continues on but there is a locked gate in half a mile and no room to turn around. The rising incline makes a switchback to the southeast.

Looking back from the peak, the route from Eagle Pass is clearly visible.

The road segment has its share of pleasures, including an evolving view of fluted Baker Peak and the ridge spanning to Silver Mountain. Go around the gate and stay on the road as it sweeps west of Eagle Pass and Point 11,900'.

To climb Baker Peak, locate the juncture of the service road and the southwest ridge of Point 11,900' at 3.9 miles. The La Plata topo marks this elevation at 11,776 feet. The drop to Puzzle Pass is about 640 feet. The ridge is rounded and the grade is gentle at first. The divide splits at 4.1 miles. Bear right on the southwest ridge or you will plunge into Lightner Creek.

Progress slows as the now rock- and tree-covered spine constricts. An old burro trail materializes at about 11,650 feet. It runs parallel to the ridgeline 50 feet off on the east side. Run it out and return to the ridge at 11,500 feet. There are several, if not many, rollers on the ridge. The steepest is the 150 foot earthen skyscraper that crashes down to Puzzle Pass at 5.0 miles, 11,140 feet.

All that remains of a miner's cabin on the pass is a stacked stone stove and remnants of the rock foundation. The Puzzle Mine was worked for

gold, silver, and lead from the 1880s through 1943. One of the veins in the Puzzle system passes right under the cabin. The most abundant ore minerals in the quartz deposit are pyrite and tetrahedrite. Artifacts are scattered throughout the area. Please leave them in place.

The approach over, climb 800 feet up the northeast ridge. Myrtle blueberry and bear scat cover the forest floor beneath old growth spruce. The incline is steep but moderated by fragments of social trail on the ridgetop. Trees give way to small talus and grass above 11,400 feet. The ridge narrows with mild exposure. Rock is well seated as you climb the natural staircase.

Pop up onto the northwest ridge. This is a wild and dramatic moment with Silver Mountain appearing in your immediate field of vision. Baker's high point is just three stony bumps away at 5.6 miles. The sweet little summit is composed of shattered, fine-grain igneous rock jutting up on angle.

Baker Peak is on the divide between the Lightner Creek watershed and the La Plata River so views are boundless. Looking east, familiar landmarks surrounding Durango are deep below and the dazzling peaks in the San Juan Mountains are integrated with the sky. Neighboring Lewis Mountain may look hulking from here but the entire ridgeline (and that's only half of it) is a delicate thread.

Silver Mountain Traverse

For years it was common to tack Baker onto the Deadwood and Silver mountains climb. Strong hikers started in La Plata City, climbed the three peaks, and then returned to the Silver-Baker saddle. They dropped through the upper basin to an abandoned wagon road along Tirbircio Creek. Another route descended on Baker's northwest ridge to the Gold King Mill. Both routes are currently off-limits because of a strip of private property at the confluence of Tirbircio Creek and the La Plata River. Therefore, if you are not going on to Silver, return as you came.

The roundtrip to Silver Mountain adds two miles with 850 feet of elevation

Two obstacles present themselves on the ridge to Silver, but are easily overcome.

gain going over and 350 feet coming back. The south side of Baker is
one big rock pile. Drop into the
saddle north of double-knobbed
Point 11,818'. The crux of the traverse is the north face of the first
hump, just beyond the small treed
saddle. It is dicey and exposed
getting around the trees on the
west side.

There is a 1989 benchmark on
the first knob. Descend on a
short razor-thin ridge and then
pitch up to Point 11,818'. The
terrain is inconsequential from
here on. A social trail down to the saddle, 5.9 miles,
11,700 feet, tracks most of the way to the crest. The krummholz gives out at
11,900 feet. A false summit is followed by a talus mound which you can
charge over or skirt around on the west.

As you are topping out on the exceedingly broad, tundra-covered summit (6.6 miles) look for a reference mark placed in 1936. The actual benchmark is missing. The voluminous, outstretched, grassy tabletop is an ideal
place to spin repeatedly in circles. Silver Mountain is visible from all the
high points in and around Durango. If a town and mountain can be wed-
ded, this is the perfect union.

Way off in the north are the San Miguel Mountains, home to the Wilson
cluster of fourteeners. The five ranked La Plata thirteeners are visible in the
northern tier of the West Block.

Retrace your steps over Baker Peak, drop down through Puzzle Pass,
mount the ridge, and return to the service road. If you'd like to see Point
11,900' and Eagle Pass, it's a quick 125-foot climb to the prominent knoll
and additional mileage is negligible. The overlook is only a few feet shorter
than Baker but to look westward you must peer through a weather station
and collection of communication towers.

SILVER MOUNTAIN, 12,496' AND DEADWOOD MOUNTAIN, 12,285'

*To see the greatness of a mountain, one must keep one's distance;
to understand its form, one must move around it; to experience its moods,
one must see it at sunrise and sunset, at noon and at midnight, in sun and
in rain, in snow and in storm, in summer and in winter and in all the other
seasons. He who can see the mountain like this comes near to the life of the
mountain, a life that is as intense and varied as that of a human being.
Such is the greatness of a mighty mountain.*

— Lama Govinda

Silver Mountain is the one peak of the La Platas that stands sentry over Durango, always visible, always drawing the eye. This is an essential climb for those who enjoy assembling a landscape puzzle that solidifies the sense of belonging to place. The hike is straightforward but somewhat arduous. The route is topped by a peaceful, tundra-covered ridge rising up and over Deadwood Mountain and culminating at the La Plata's namesake peak.

ABOUT THIS HIKE
Distance: 10.1 miles
Elevation Gain: 4,350 feet
Time: 6:00 to 7:30
Route Surface: jeep track, social trail
Class: 2
Exposure: none
Navigation: moderate

Travel

Measure distance from the junction of US 160 and La Plata Canyon Road, CR 124. After passing the hamlet of Mayday the road turns to smooth dirt at 4.6 miles. The 2WD accessible trailhead is at 7.8 miles. Park on the right at placard displays for historic La Plata City.

Route

La Plata City was founded in the early 1880s. As the residential and commercial hub of the La Plata mining frontier, it had a peak population of

CALTOPO
N
CR 124
Trailhead 9,140'
9600
9400
10000
Bragdon
10200
FSR 797
10400
Middle Mountain
River
9600
10000
11,078'
Ridge
10600
10800
Burnt Timber Creek
Snowslide Creek
10800
10000
11,000
11700
11,000
10400
Schwilke
10200
11600
11800
Schwilke Creek
10800
Ridge
12,285'
11000
Deadwood Mountain
L A
12,000
10800
P L A T A
11,200
11400
11600
Paine Ridge
11400
Baker Peak
9,949'
12,000
12,496'
Silver Mountain
2000
10800

1,000. Ore deposits were low grade and limited so mining operations were not profitable. By the 1930s, the humble homesteads, post office, school, and grocery were boarded up or destroyed and the people moved on.

From the large parking area, elevation 9,140 feet, walk down FSR 797 toward the La Plata River. Bear right, passing a primitive camping area. Ford the river directly across from the road which punches up the opposite bank. When the water is low you can hop to the other side on boulders and logs. However, wading across during spring run-off or the monsoon can be hazardous.

Note the social trail branching onto the ridge from the road intersection.

Walk up the steep, earthen, 4WD track as it steadily progresses east while staying south of Neptune Creek. In early season, fallen trees are frequently strewn across the road. Frankly, this extended switchbacking segment can feel tedious and you will welcome the company of a friend. Or, enjoy the rhapsody of woodland flowers such as sunny and sprightly heart leaf arnica.

Old mining tracks branch off. Stay on the main road for one and a half to two hours. At 3.3 miles, 11,660 feet, the road splits and there are US Forest Service signs prohibiting further vehicle travel in both directions. The ridgeline social trail begins here and is serviceable all the way to Deadwood's crest. The rounded, wooded ridge is somewhat steep but pleasant.

Rise through the krummholz and emerge into the alpine on Deadwood's west ridge. Thus begins one of the most exceptional ridge hikes in the La Platas. The sight lines are limitless and the route to the summit is obvious on broken talus.

Crest the shallow curvature of Deadwood Mountain at 3.8 miles. Net elevation gain is 3,200 feet thus far so a big portion of the day's climbing is accomplished. Look southwest to appealing Ohwiler Ridge and directly south to

Baldy Peak, 10,868', the most southerly mountain in the range.

Silver Mountain is commanding, and traversing the one-and-a-quarter-mile sinuous, undulating ridge is pure pleasure. This final segment will take 45 minutes to an hour each way. Before launching, consider your safety. These are weather-making mountains and electrical storms blow up in minutes.

Alpine flowers delight along the way. Mid-summer, magenta paintbrush are profuse as well as mouse ear chickweed, old man of the mountain, moss campion, deep-rooted spring beauty, sky pilot, purple fringe, and even tiny patches of forget-me-nots. Get down on your knees and inhale alpine phlox for an intense whiff of euphoria. Scrutinize Silver Basin on the east side of the ridge for the local elk herd grazing in the tundra.

Clamber over a roller and descend to the saddle on a trail just to the north of the ridge top. From the low point between the peaks at 12,020 feet, 500 feet of climbing remains. The final push

up the west ridge social trail is on small talus and tundra.

The summit of Silver Mountain is as broad and welcoming as you imagine it to be when seeing it from Durango. It will take anywhere from two and a half to four hours to reach the crest from the trailhead with 3,850 feet of gain over 5.05 miles. The Silver Benchmark is missing but a reference mark placed in 1936 remains.

The observation point provides a full-circle spin through the ranges of southern Colorado. Directly across La Plata Canyon is the Four Peak Traverse. Moving right is The Knife spanning from West Babcock to Spiller Peak. In the northern tier are the five ranked La Plata thirteeners. Most locals climb Silver Mountain to satisfy a curiosity about their landmark mountain and to look back from the opposite perspective.

Traverse to Baker Peak, 11,949'

For years we tacked Baker Peak onto our Deadwood and Silver climb. We'd start in La Plata City, climb the three peaks, return to the Silver-Baker

saddle (11,700 feet) and descend Tirbircio Creek. That bailout is now off-limits because of a small strip of private property at the confluence of Tirbircio Creek and the La Plata River. Therefore, if you want to climb Baker from Silver–lovely but not ranked–you will have to do it as an out-and-back.

Relax on the flowery lawn of the peak while regarding the less comforting challenges nearby.

The traverse adds two miles total and 1,200 feet of vertical. Alternatively, climb Baker from Eagle Pass and Puzzle Pass and throw in the traverse to Silver. Please see that hike description for a discussion of the moderately exposed crux on the north face of Point 11,818' on the traverse.

To return to the trailhead, you must reclimb Deadwood. It looks and feels like a ranked peak but doesn't quite make the 300-foot cut with just 265 feet of prominence. However, given the rollers there is over 400 feet of vertical back to the neighboring summit.

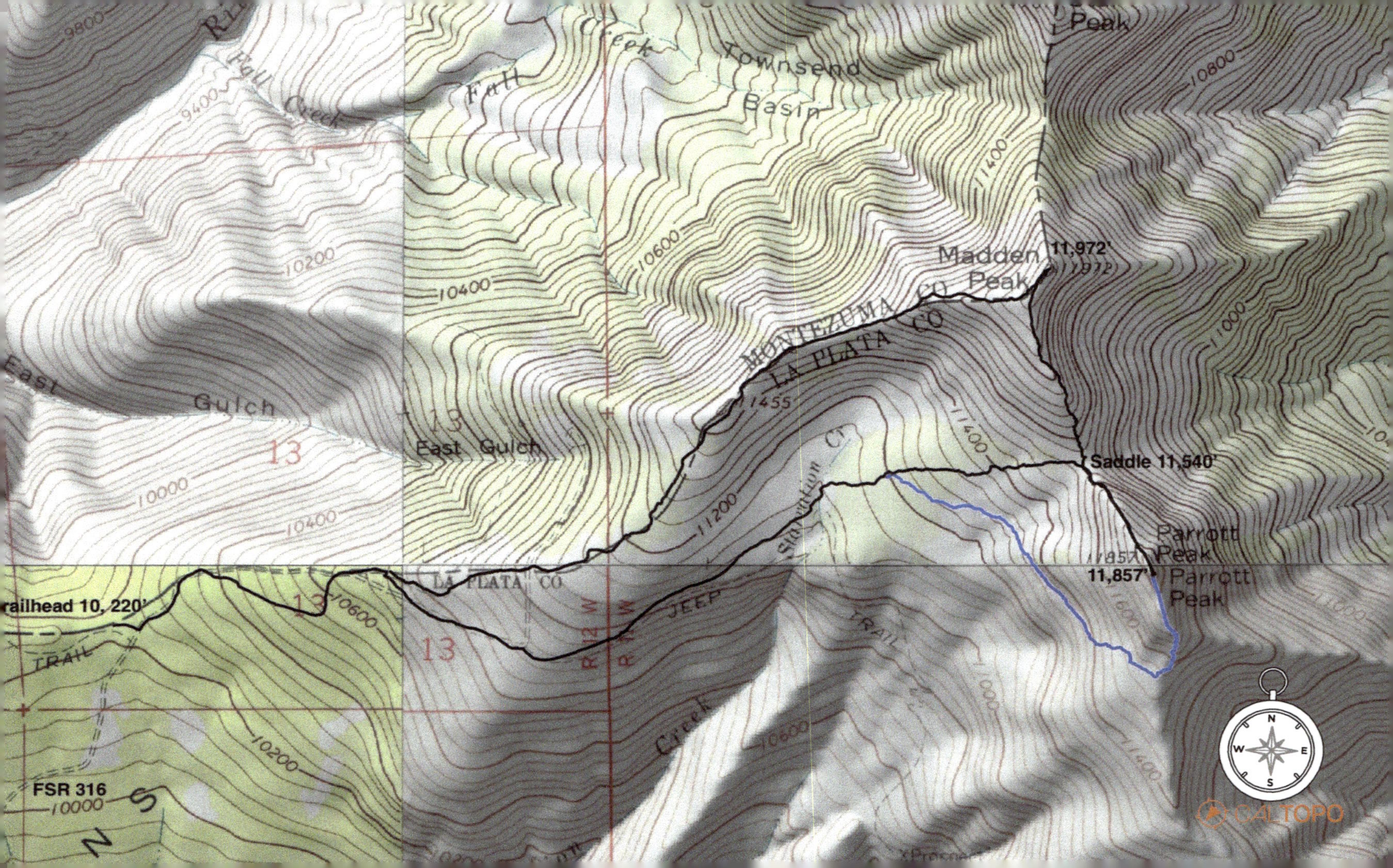

Rico
9800
9400
Fall Creek
Townsend Basin
Peak
10800
10200
10400
10600
11400
10000
Madden Peak 11,972'
1972
11,000
MONTEZUMA CO
LA PLATA CO
East Gulch
13
East Gulch
1455
10000
10400
Starvation Cr
11400
Saddle 11,540'
11200
Parrott Peak
11,857'
Parrott Peak
Trailhead 10,220'
13
10600
LA PLATA CO
R. 12 W
R. 11 W
JEEP
TRAIL
11,600
11000
TRAIL
FSR 316
10000
N S
10200
Creek
10600
11400
N
W E
S
CALTOPO

MADDEN PEAK, 11,972'
AND PARROTT PEAK, 11,857'
WESTERN APPROACH

Faeries, come take me out of this dull world,
For I would ride with you upon the wind,
Run on the top of the disheveled tide,
And dance upon the mountains like a flame.

— W.B. Yeats

This hike offers early-season access to the western La Platas when snow lingers on the peaks. Or, walk through autumn splendor when the fiery hues of the aspen quicken the way. This is the easiest and fastest route to the two summits in the southwest corner of the range. The stem and loop utilizes abandoned jeep tracks for much of the distance. Ascend into the full glory of the mountains via the west ridge of Madden Peak while the Colorado Plateau's voluminous, yawning space splays out to the southwest.

ABOUT THIS HIKE
Distance: 5.0 miles
Elevation Gain: 2,100 feet
Time: 3:00 to 5:00
Route Surface: jeep track, trail, talus
Class: 2
Exposure: none
Navigation: moderate
Additional Maps: Thompson Park; Hesperus, Colorado 7.5' USGS Quads

Travel

This approach requires a 4WD vehicle with high clearance. The access road is off of US Hwy 160, roughly 22 miles west of Durango and six miles east of Mancos. At the top of "Mancos Hill," mile marker 61.8, turn north onto signed Madden Peak Road and measure distance from there. The gravel road narrows and turns to dirt as it becomes FSR 316 at one mile, where a track goes off to the right. Stay straight and gain elevation quickly. The primitive dirt road has deep ruts and may be impassible when wet. The surface is rocky for long stretches. At 6.9 miles, FSR 353 branches left

(closed). Continue straight, passing over a cattle guard. The track descends with a view of the west flank of the La Platas. At 8.0 miles, pass a trailhead on the right with a faded sign. This trail is not helpful for this hike. At 8.2 miles, the road splits at a Y. Take the right branch for a short distance to a parking area and circular turn-around in a lovely pastoral spot.

Route

Walk east from the parking area, elevation 10,220 feet, on a good trail for about 100 feet to a closed 4WD road and turn left. Make a mental note of this location for your return. The lovely dirt track, free of rock, holds to the softly rounded west ridge of Madden Peak. The path climbs steeply through an aspen forest with a few coniferous companions. In the spring, glacier lilies, spring beauties, and buttercups, abundant at the edges of snow patches, yield to columbine and bluebells. Ignore the downhill tracks that branch off to the right.

At 0.6 mile, 10,740 feet, an equally prominent dirt road branches right at a shallow angle going uphill. This initiates the loop which may be done in either direction. If you wish to climb Parrott Peak first, take the right-hand two-track until it is below the Parrott-Madden saddle. To climb Madden Peak

first, continue straight, steeply up, staying on the ridge.

Proceeding straight ahead, the road soon leads onto a wide-open grassy hillside, transitioning to a single-track. Big views open to the west. Look back on Mesa Verde, Sleeping Ute Mountain, and the small town of Mancos. Enter a fir-spruce forest at one mile where snow stubbornly hangs on into June.

At 11,460 feet, emerge from the trees. It is an exhilarating moment when both

peaks come into view. The social trail leads onto the ridgetop where the view corridor opens to the north and colorful Helmet Peak. Multiple shallow adits along the ridge are associated with the Kiabab Mine worked in 1936. A group of unpatented claims cover the ridge between Starvation Creek and the East Mancos River but no ore was produced.

A large cairn marks the beginning of the off-trail portion of the hike. The route holds to the ridgeline from here to the summit. Ascend on well-seated talus with just a few unstable blocks to negotiate. In June, you may well be climbing on top of a snow cornice. Sastrugi and sun cups help with traction but stay well away from the overhanging edge.

Alpine flowers nestled in tundra cover the dome of the mountain, thriving under a great wash of light. Early bloomers include alp lily on slender stems with six elegant petals, brilliant pink moss campion hovering over the ground, and robust old man of the mountain. Minuartia is an abundant

alpine plant forming a dense green mat. It has a profusion of delicate, tiny white five-petaled flowers. Sky pilot has also perfected adaptation to its high, dry, and windy world, producing dazzling ball-shaped clusters of tubular blue-purple flowers.

Crest Madden Peak at 2.0 miles after 1,760 feet of climbing. There is a commanding view of the majority of La Plata peaks from the tall cairn gracing the massive summit. The range falls down and away to the west, allowing unobstructed observation of the premier landmarks defining the Four Corners region.

To reach Parrott Peak, descend the south ridge of Madden while walking on thin plates of clinking igneous stone. In half a mile reach the Madden-Parrott saddle, elevation 11,540 feet. From here, it is a 317-foot rise over 0.3 mile to the summit. Locate a social trail that pitches up west of some minor cliffs before making for the ridgetop.

Parrott is more than it appears; there are two rollers on the summit ridge. Crest the southernmost prominence on the West Block of the La Plata Mountains at 2.8 miles. There is something so sweet about this little, stone-splashed peak in its all-important position. A long stretch of Highway 160 is to the

south and from there the Colorado Plateau lies in the great beyond. In the north, the San Juan Mountains are the thinnest line.

The north ridge of Parrott looks intimidating but is graced by a helpful social trail.

Ridge purists may descend on Parrott's south ridge, indicated on the map with a blue line. This alternate option adds 0.3 mile. On this route, upon reaching a weather station at timberline, pivot and walk northwest in a descending traverse across a vast and tedious talus field to rejoin the standard route.

For the easiest trek back to the trailhead, return down the north ridge to the saddle. Descend due west through a friendly, uncluttered forest. In half a mile, encounter Starvation Creek at elevation 11,100 feet. In contrast with the historical name, marsh marigold, the happiest flower of them all, gathers around the stream. As snow recedes, glacier lilies thrive in this location.

Hold your altitude and you will encounter an old jeep track just beyond the creek. Follow the road southwest. Judging from tracks, this road is more popular with elk than with humans. At 4.2 miles, come to a T intersection and continue west. This is just before the aspen treeline. Close the loop at 4.4 miles and turn left to return to the trailhead.

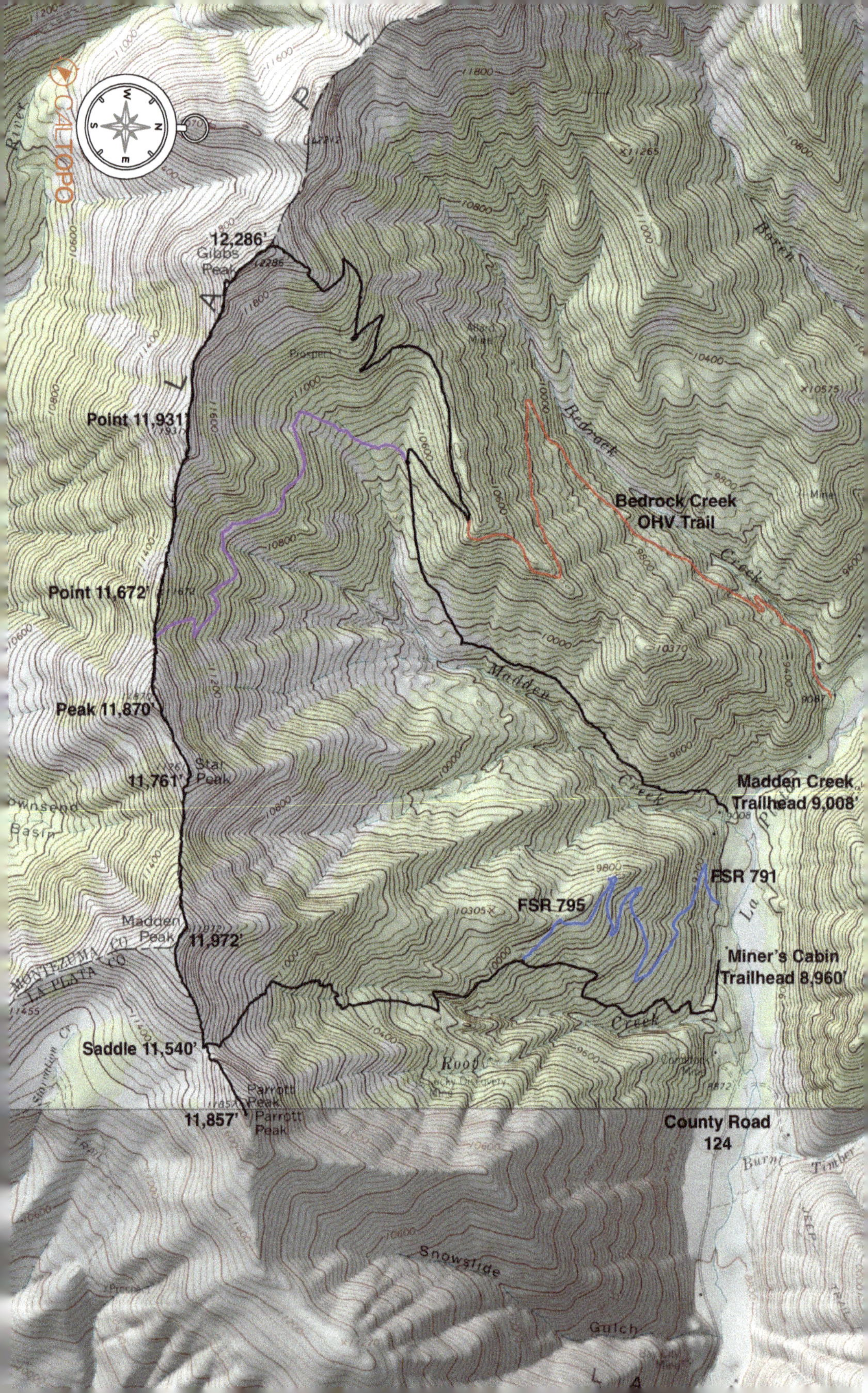

CALTOPO
River
12,286'
Glads Peak
Point 11,931'
Point 11,672'
Peak 11,870'
11,761'
Star Peak
Townsend Basin
Madden Peak
11,972'
Saddle 11,540'
11,857'
Parrott Peak
MONTEZUMA CO
LA PLATA CO
Prospect
Bedrock Creek OHV Trail
Madden Creek
Bedrock Creek
Madden Creek Trailhead 9,008'
FSR 791
FSR 795
Miner's Cabin Trailhead 8,960'
La Plata River
Kroeger
Snowslide Gulch
County Road 124
Burnt Timber
LA PLATA

FOUR PEAK TRAVERSE:
PARROTT, 11,857'; MADDEN; 11,972'; STAR, 11,761'; & GIBBS, 12,286'

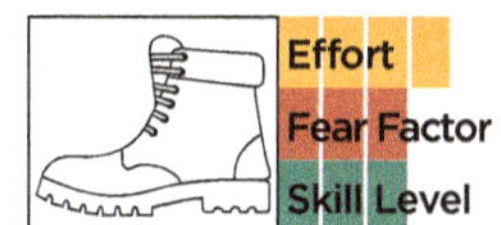

Something hidden. Go and find it.
Go and look behind the Ranges—
Something lost behind the Ranges.
Lost and waiting for you. Go!

— Rudyard Kipling

An extraordinary and sustained ridge line traverse occupies the southern portion of the elevated West Block. Take advantage of the divide's evolving panorama as you climb up and over four ranked summits and three additional prominences. To the southwest, a vast field of open space melds into the blue distance. Northward, the ridge undulates, advancing ever higher, peak beyond peak. Challenges on the primarily off-trail circuit include steep slopes, loose talus, substantial elevation gain, and notoriously skittish footing encircling Gibbs Peak.

ABOUT THIS HIKE
Distance: 9.7 miles
Elevation Gain: 4,750 feet of climbing
Time: 6:30 to 9:00
Route Surface: jeep track, trail, primarily off-trail, talus, friable and loose rock
Class: 2+
Exposure: moderate
Navigation: challenging

Travel

Measure distance from the junction of US 160 and La Plata Canyon Road, CR 124. After passing the hamlet of Mayday the road turns to smooth dirt at 4.6 miles. Park on the right at 6.3 miles. Watch for a Forest Service Miner's Cabin Campground sign just past a chain-link fence.

Route

Four principal lateral routes head west from the floor of La Plata Canyon and make for the ridge line. All four will be discussed in reference to the

Cornhusk lillies carpet the floor of Root Creek basin in the spring.

route indicated with a black line on the map. This description goes clockwise around the circuit for the most dramatic views but you could reverse the direction.

Miner's Cabin Trail, Black-Line Route

The circuit hike begins from the pullout at Miner's Cabin, elevation 8,960 feet, and climbs through Root Creek basin to the saddle between Parrott Peak and Madden Peak. Walk a few paces down La Plata Canyon Road and take the first 4WD track on the west side. The initial segment is steep and fast. Enter an aspen and Douglas fir wood. At 0.2 mile take the right fork. In spring, red columbine, white violet, and orange sneezeweed blossom in the road.

At 0.9 mile, 9,920 feet, reach the unsigned junction with FSR 795. Prior to the T intersection the abandoned track has been deliberately disguised with slash. If you plan to return this way, make a mental note of this juncture.

Walk west on FSR 795 and cross the west fork of Root Creek at 1.2 miles, 10,040 feet. Rise out of the drainage and locate a faint two-track bearing west on the south side of the tributary. The road crosses two streams before ending at 1.7 miles, 10,600 feet. Climb a steep open slope for 500 feet, watching for a large grove of old-growth spruce on your left with a tangle of massive above-ground roots.

Locate an old miner's trail just above the stand of trees. The scrappy trail does a rising traverse southwest cutting nicely across a talus field for 0.1 mile. Push through a krummholz barrier and out onto an open slope. From here, it is a steep slog with good footing to the saddle at 2.2 miles, elevation 11,540 feet.

Green Bus Trail, Blue–Line Route

An alternative access to Root Creek basin begins from CR 124 and FSR 791, 0.2 mile up the road from Miner's Cabin. The Forest Service sign refers to this as the Madden Trail but locals call it the Green Bus Trail even though the picturesque bus that was parked beside the county road is long gone. The jeep track rises gradually with long switchbacks through a lovely aspen forest to the junction with FSR 795 at 1.6 miles. Turn left, and walk another half mile to the west fork crossing. This option adds almost a mile.

Parrott Peak, 11,857'

Parrott Peak is a 0.3 mile spur to the south with a rise of 317 feet. This is the only time you will double up steps on the loop. The minor cliffs on Parrott's north face are bypassed on the west. Locate a braided social trail that pitches up on talus for about 80 feet before gaining the ridge crest.

Climb over two rollers and top out on the summit cone. The southernmost peak in the West Block affords a unique perspective on the compact range. Across the La Plata River canyon, the skirts of mountains standing shoulder to shoulder are clothed in a forest-green tinged with purple. Unbounded views of the Four Corners showcase Point Lookout at Mesa Verde National Park, Shiprock, Sleeping Ute Mountain, and the Abajo and La Sal mountains.

Madden Peak, 11,972'

Return to the saddle and mount 432 feet up Madden's broad and pleasurable southern back on well-seated stone blocks and slabs. The mountain is extraordinary for its unbroken simplicity which serves to highlight the immense span of measureless space beyond the range. Arrive at the four-foot, stacked summit cairn 3.2 miles into the hike.

Snow tends to dissipate from the approach to both Parrott and Madden in early summer when taller peaks remain under cover. The relatively short hike through Root Creek basin to the pair is an annual warmup for locals. From here, the ensuing northward ridge walk and lateral back to the trailhead is a considerable commitment of both time and difficulty. If the weather is threatening or two peaks are enough for one day, this is your turnaround.

Star Peak, 11,761'

The array of peaks in the north—some perilous sharp spires, others curvilinear—are the ridge walker's ever-present skyline companions. The north slope of Madden is composed of chipped and broken talus, indicative of the treadway for the next couple of miles.

Give up over 500 feet to the Madden-Star saddle, descending into stands of timber where deep snow pockets may be found well into summer. The flat rocks on Star's south incline sound like plates breaking underfoot. Crest the roller at 3.7 miles. It is a curiosity that Star is singled out and named. It is not a ranked summit whereas Peak 11,870' to its immediate north makes the cut with a rise of 330 feet.

One of the most challenging pitches on the ridge leads to unnamed Peak 11,870'.

Peak 11,870'

Drop an inconsequential 40 feet and then pitch steeply up the stoney south slope of Peak 11,870'. Top out on the summit dome at 4.0 miles. From the massive rock pile that serves as a summit cairn, Lone Cone, the westernmost peak in the San Juan Mountains, is visible on the northern horizon.

Escape Option, Purple-Line Route

The scree on the north side of Peak 11,870' makes a delightful tinkling melody. The saddle between Peak 11,870' and Point 11,672' is a bailout location, depicted on the map with a purple line. If the weather is threatening or you would rather not

climb Gibbs, you can descend to the Madden Creek Trail from here. Do a descending traverse northeast off-trail. The footing is good on the steep hillside. Intersect an abandoned jeep track and follow it north into the Madden Creek headwater basin. Descend east on a broad avalanche path to another old mining track where you will intersect the black-line route. This choice requires some navigation savvy and map-reading ability.

Point 11,931'

From the bailout saddle, rise up and over inconsequential Point 11,672' on a tundra-stone mix. Approaching Point 11,931', a short social trail initiates at 11,800 feet and wanders up through the rough spots. Top the rocky knob at 5.1 miles. From here, the remainder of the ridge traverse and climb to the fourth and final peak is clearly visible.

Gibbs Peak, 12,286'

The rocky ridge constricts just enough to be exhilarating. Now is the time to pay more attention to your footing than the scenery. The spine

soon widens and opens onto a gravel field rising to a false summit. Descend into a minor saddle at 12,080 feet.

A cliff bars further passage on the divide. Move west then scramble up skittish and rotten rock to regain the ridge at first opportunity. Test holds on the deceivingly friable stone. There is mild exposure on the sliding scree. The summit ridge is glorious. It is wide enough to provide security and beaten down from use.

Crest Gibbs Peak, the highest and most difficult mountain on the hike at 5.6 miles after a whopping 4,700 feet of vertical gain. Look south to review the entire traverse. Heart-stopping drama is provided by the northern backdrop of severe and ragged peaks spanning from Hesperus Mountain to East Babcock Peak.

The summit blocks of Gibbs and Burwell Peak, its neighbor to the north, are a tawny rust color and the rock composition is altogether different than the surrounding mountains. Sorely tested hikers have referred to the stone as garbage rock. Geological surveys, on the other hand, have identified brecciated rock impregnated with auriferous pyrite.

Madden Creek Trail

Work carefully down the east ridge of Gibbs searching out dependable holds while being mindful of the exposure. After 150 feet the grade decreases and a social trail develops.

Stay on the spine until you intersect an old mining track 0.3 mile off the top at 11,780 feet and turn left. Be sure to nail this trail. It does one switchback and then at 6.2 miles, 11,480 feet, contacts Gibbs Road, officially named the Bedrock Creek OHV Trail. A cairn marks this important junction. Turn right. At 6.9 miles the road branches right and then left. Continue straight, staying on the main track.

At 7.3 miles, 10,700 feet, the black-line route leaves Gibbs Road. If you've had enough route finding for one day, stay on the main road, the red-line route. It winds lazily back to CR 124 at Bedrock Creek, adding 1.3 miles to the total distance. To finish on the Madden Creek Trail, make a hard right turn onto a secondary rocky track bearing northwest. The track switchbacks south and intersects the purple-line escape route at 10,500 feet.

Continue walking south on the abandoned jeep track surrendering to dandelions and grass. At 8.2 miles, 9,920 feet, enter a glade of aspen carved

A lonely fortune seeker once carved his true wish onto the only medium available at the lower end of the Madden Creek Trail.

with historic arborglyphs. Make a left onto the Madden Creek Trail. (The road ends at Madden Creek if you miss the turn.)

The maintained dirt path descends through a forest of healthy and stately aspen. In autumn, the trees and trailside thimbleberry light the way to a golden finish.

Approaching CR 124 at 9.2 miles, turn around to locate an arborglyph, the namesake of this "Naked Lady Trail." The footpath spills out onto CR 124 just north of the Madden Creek crossing. Walk half a mile down the county road to the Miner's Cabin trailhead parking.

BURWELL PEAK, 12,664'

Whatever you think you can do or dream you can, begin it.
Boldness has genius, power, and magic in it.

— Goethe

With a rise of 164 feet off the Spiller Peak saddle, Burwell is not a ranked summit but it is the southern highpoint on the rim of Boren Creek Basin. Burwell is isolated by a vertical walled notch just north of the amber-colored summit block. While it is arguably the most approachable peak of the Boren group, it is not trivial. An extremely steep ascent leads to even more challenge several hundred feet below the summit. The rock is friable, but there are enough good holds for an enjoyable push to the crest with its far-flung views to the west and intimate visual of its even more radical neighbors.

ABOUT THIS HIKE
Distance: 6.2 miles
Elevation Gain: 3,550 feet
Total Time: 5:00 to 6:00
Route Surface: jeep track, primarily off-trail, steep slopes, loose and friable rock, resistant soil
Class: 2+
Exposure: moderate
Navigation: challenging

Travel

Measure distance from the junction of US 160 and La Plata Canyon Road, CR 124. After passing the hamlet of Mayday the road turns to smooth dirt at 4.6 miles. Park in a pullout on the right at 8.1 miles, just past Boren Creek and before FSR 794. Enthusiasts with a dedicated 4WD, short wheelbase vehicle may drive up the steep, rocky, narrow two-track 1.7 miles to the split from FSR 794.

Route

From the pullout, elevation 9,240 feet, walk up La Plata Canyon Road about 200 feet and start hiking northwest up Boren Creek Road, FSR 794. Lovely aspen woods enhance the cobbly experience. Hop across Shaw Gulch

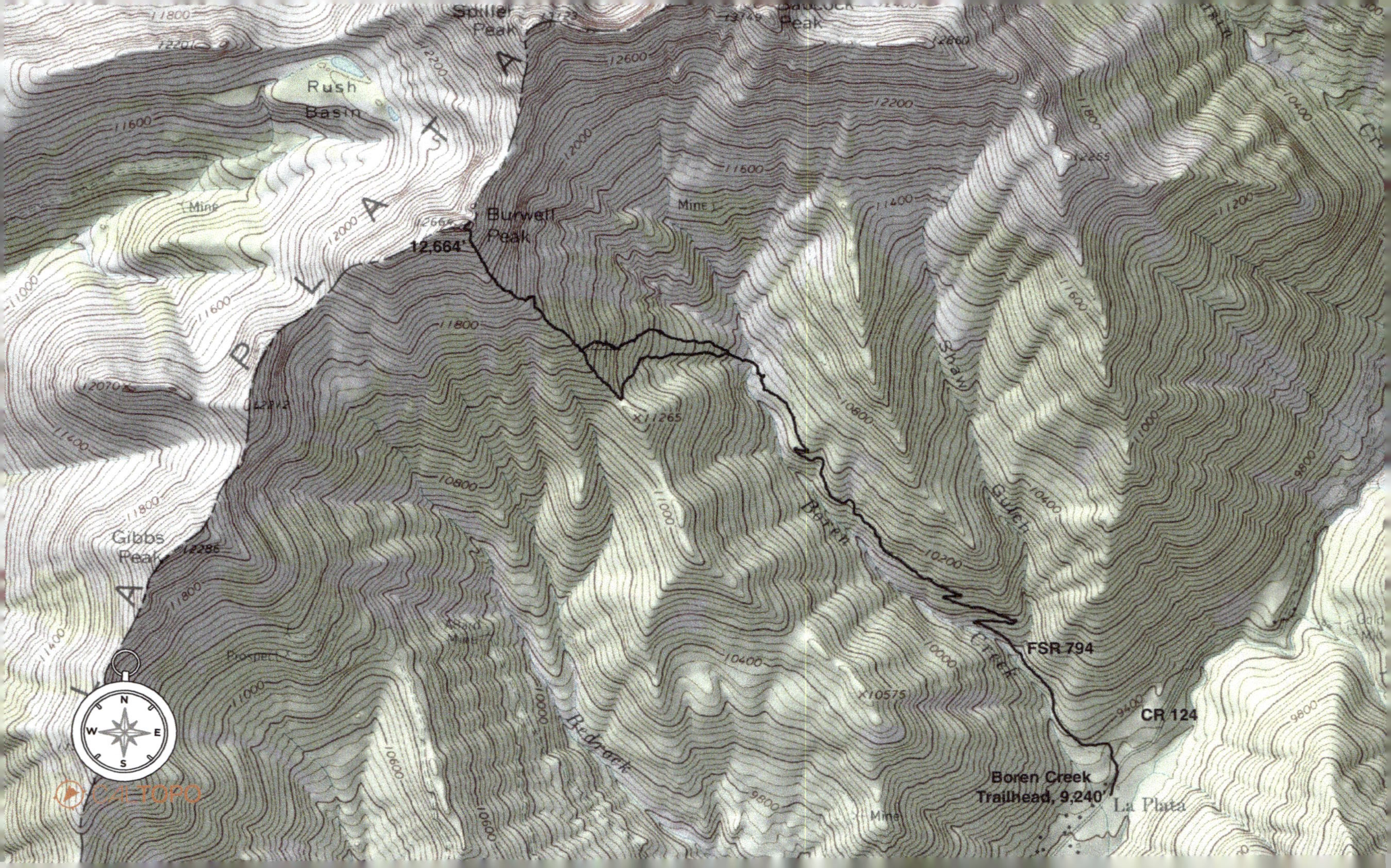

Spiller Peak
Sawtooth Peak
Rush Basin
Mine
Burwell Peak
12,664'
Mine
12,265
Shaw
PLATA
Gibbs Peak
12,286
Boren
Gulch
Prospect
Mine
FSR 794
X 10575
CR 124
Boren Creek Trailhead, 9,240'
La Plata
N W S E
CALTOPO

Above: A ring of challenging sentinels surround the headwaters of Boren Creek.

Left: The obvious notch prevents access to Burwell from the saddle with Spiller Peak, necessitating the approach from the southeast ridge.

at 0.5 mile. At 1.7 miles, elevation 10,480 feet, leave the jeep track, taking the left hand spur. This is the first branch off FSR 794 so you can't miss it.

The spur ends in a clearing on a platform above Boren Creek. Water falls over stone in the center of Boren Creek Basin. Some of the most challenging mountains in the La Plata range ring the bowl: Burwell Peak; Spiller

Peak; the Knife; and West, Middle, and East Babcock peaks.

Before initiating the ascent, walk northwest across the platform and look over your options for gaining the southeast ridge of Burwell. No matter the route, it is an arduous effort. Climb almost 2,200 feet from creek to summit in just one mile.

Locate a game trail down to Boren Creek, elevation 10,500 feet. It is common for the watercourse to be buried under avalanche debris long into summer. In autumn, pause to eat gooseberries and search out an uncommon Indian warrior lousewort.

For the brute force route to the ridge—the more northern of the two tracks on the map—cross the creek, climb west up the open avalanche path, and then veer away from the gully. Deadfall in the spruce woods is not an impediment and intermittent game trails assist. Intersect the southeast ridge at about 11,500 feet.

The more elegant route adds 0.1 mile but you will spend more time on the ridge and less time on the high-angle slope. Start up the slide path and

then track above the gully in the trees to its north. Cross the channel at its head, elevation 11,040 feet. Do a rising traverse southwest to the saddle. Angling away from the mountain is a little counter-intuitive but the gradient is tempered throughout the climb. Reach the saddle at 11,220 feet, where a post stands in a pile of rocks.

After gaining the ridge, the grade eases somewhat in the tundra. When stone takes over, be on the lookout for the "Rock Stack" at 11,880 feet. This is the most significant obstacle on the hike. Flank the outcrop on the right. Hug the wall to control the exposure.

Immediately past the outcrop, make a sharp left onto a social trail and return to the ridge. The scant trail continues up the open ridgeline composed of gravel and scree. Pass through a short krummholz band, where the determined tree tops are flat and spreading against the cold.

Manganese oxide coats the rock with an ebony sheen. As the pitch steepens, marbles and cobbles slide on resistant soil. Groups need to be

wary of rockfall on the upper mountain. Route finding is a game on the summit block where the safest options are to the right of the ridgeline. Near the crest textured bedrock slabs are more continuous. Test all holds in the friable stone.

Crest the small cone with sharp-edged sitting rocks at 3.1 miles. For most, the 3,500 foot climb will take the better part of three hours. La Plata summits fall sharply away into the embrace of the American West where the field of vision is never-ending. Parrott Peak anchors the south end of the West Block. Coming north are Madden, Star, and Gibbs peaks. While it is tempting to turn the Four Peak Traverse into something truly massive, there isn't a way to get from Gibbs to Burwell without dropping radically off the ridge to the west.

Wonder amplifies as your gaze swings north to the bodacious peaks ringing the Boren Creek Basin. Use caution picking your way gingerly off the summit block and retrace your steps to La Plata Canyon Road.

BALDY PEAK, 10,866'

> *There was a time when meadow, grove, and stream*
> *The earth, and every common sight*
> *To me did seem*
> *Appareled in celestial light*
> *The glory and the freshness of a dream.*
>
> — William Wordsworth

The lowest peak in the range ironically requires the highest effort to summit. Baldy is only two miles east of Mayday but you cannot get there from the village because of private property limitations. This all-day hike approaches from the east and is wholly contained within Perins Peak State Wildlife Area and San Juan National Forest. Aspen groves give way to an expansive spherical summit, the southern terminus of the La Plata Mountains. Yes, this is a long and rugged hike to a relatively low peak but that is a good deal of its charm; watch for uncommon flowers along the way. Proven fitness and astute navigation skills are essential. Carry sufficient food and water for a full day of hiking.

ABOUT THIS HIKE
Distance: 16.0 miles
Elevation Gain: 5,150 feet
Total Time: 9:30 to 11:30
Route Surface: trail, off-trail, jeep track, brush
Class: 2
Exposure: none
Navigation: most challenging
Additional Maps: Durango West; Hesperus, Colorado 7.5' USGS Quads
Winter Closure: Public access is prohibited in Perins Peak State Wildlife Area during the closure period, December 1 through April 15. Dogs must be on leash.

Travel

Begin measuring distance at the US 160 and US 550 junction in Durango. Drive west on US 160. Turn right on Lightner Creek Road, CR 207, at 3.3 miles. Take a soft right on Dry Fork Road, CR 208, at 4.4 miles. At 6.3 miles take the left fork. Swing left into the generous parking lot at 6.5 miles. The dirt road is prone to potholes but 2WD vehicles should make the trailhead.

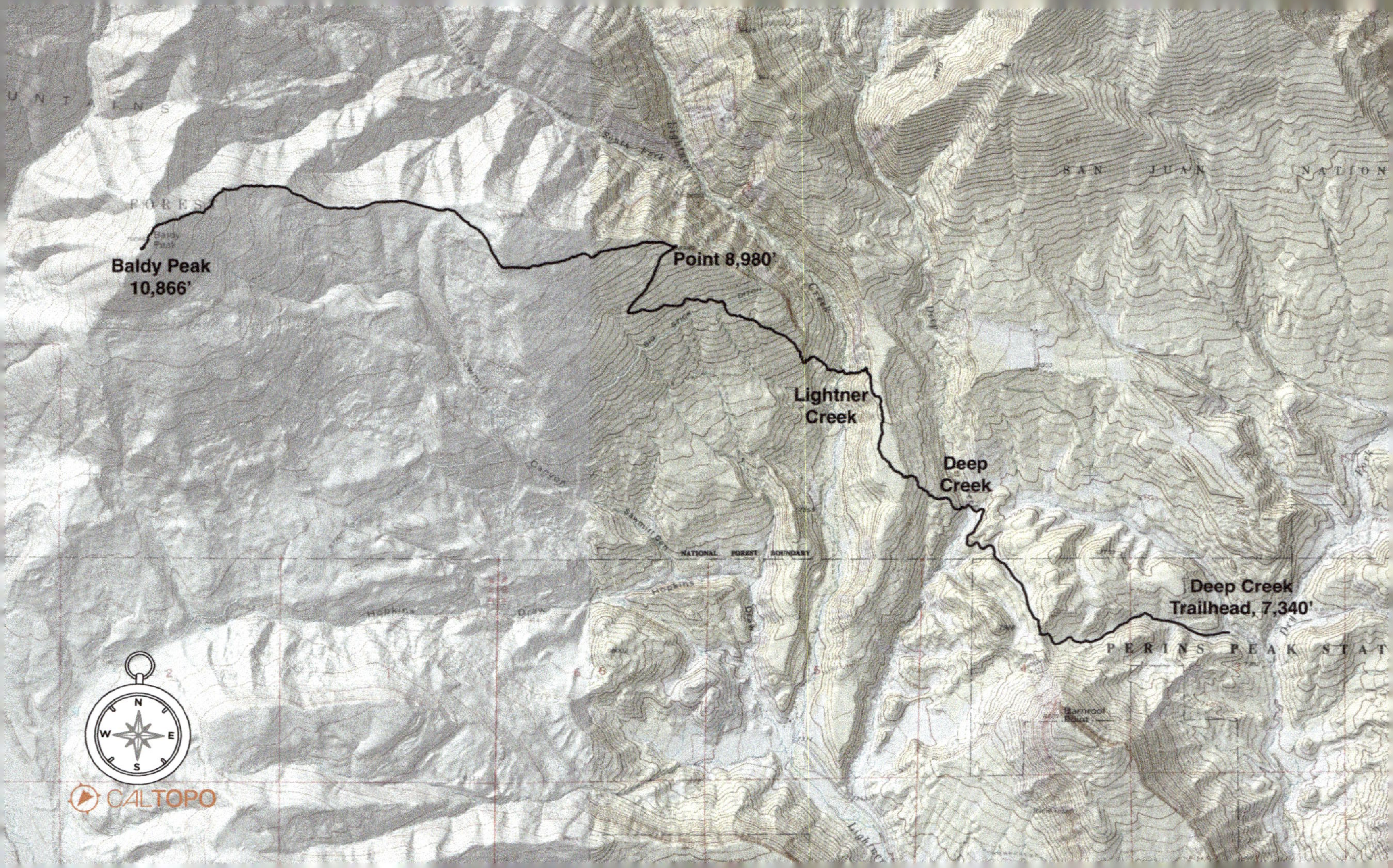

Baldy Peak
10,866'
Point 8,980'
Lightner
Creek
Deep
Creek
Deep Creek
Trailhead, 7,340'
N
W E
S
CALTOPO

Route

From the Deep Creek Trailhead, elevation 7,340 feet, walk west along a tributary of Dry Fork on a well-defined trail within Perins Peak State Wildlife Area managed by Colorado Parks and Wildlife. The path climbs softly through ponderosa and aspen and passes a prize-winning Gambel oak. Hawthorn trees blossom profusely in early summer. The trail rises to a low pass directly under the north slopes of Barnroof Point at 1.0 mile, 7,780 feet.

Pause and get your bearings. Looking northwest, Deep Creek is in the first depression. A glacial moraine separates Deep Creek from Lightner Creek. Next, is the southeast flank of Baldy. Silver Mountain rises stately on the skyline. The trail turns north onto a low ridge. Follow it for about ten paces and then branch left onto a descending path across a lush meadow. If the treadway becomes obscure, hold a northwest trajectory into a draw. Cross into the San Juan National Forest at 1.5 miles. Please close the gate.

The footpath passes through a stand of old growth ponderosa, swings down into a cottonwood-framed meadow at Deep Creek, and ends at 2.0 miles, 7,500 feet. Jump across the creek and bushwhack northwest up the

In spite of having the goal in sight (center-left), the first view of your route makes the challenge clear.

east-facing slope of the moraine. Gain the ridge at 7,940 feet and walk north through glades and stands of Gamble oak.

Persevere through thickets of oak and snowberry until you reach elevation 8,040 feet. You must attain this elevation to avoid private land. It is helpful to carry a GPS unit that delineates the public-private land boundaries. The west side of the moraine is pitched and troubled with cliffs. Plummet down at the limit of possibility to Lightner Creek at 3.3 miles, 7,660 feet. Fording the creek can be hazardous during spring runoff or during the summer monsoon. A knee-deep barefoot wade is not uncommon.

Now you must climb 800 feet northwest off-trail. Mount steeply through massive blocks that tumbled from the Dakota Sandstone scarp. Search out a manageable break in the cliff band.

Intersect an abandoned mining road that ascends the east flank of the mountain. It winds for miles up to the Texas Chief Mine above the South Fork of Lightner Creek. With any luck, you will hit the track where the Big Stick Ditch crosses the road at 4.1 miles, 8,500 feet. Make sure you are on the road, not the ditch. The road does a major switchback to the northeast. At Point 8,980' it cuts westward. From this vantage point you can see Silver and Lewis mountains and look down onto the Entrada Sandstone slab that projects from Barnroof Point.

There are occasional glimpses of Baldy Peak through resplendent aspen. Four card suits were carved into one trunk long ago. This is the land of big trees. Elderly ponderosa have exceptionally wide girths. Limber pines are distinguished by their large cones.

The track passes an open fenceline at 9,500 feet and disappears in a spacious meadow. Hold your bearing and the road will reappear on the other side.

At 6.7 miles, 9,640 feet, the long approach is over. Leave the road branching left onto a trail and begin the east ridge ascent. Just shy of

10,000 feet, a mile off the top, the footpath veers left. Leave the trail, staying on the east ridge. Walk through a mixed forest with some deadfall. Five hundred feet from the crest, emerge onto a steep grassy slope enhanced with scattered spruce.

Round the spherical cap of the luminous summit, tucked under the purview of Deadwood and Silver mountains. From the curve of the mountaintop the westward view opens to Sleeping Ute and Shiprock. Baldy Peak feels quintessentially Western and shares a reciprocal kinship with the town of Durango, visible in the southeast. The Needle Mountains and Mountain View Crest are an entire mountain range away but startle in their visual proximity.

On the return, be mentally and physically prepared for the 400-foot climb out of Lightner Creek and the 250-foot gradual ascent from Deep Creek to the base of Barnroof Point.

This is one of the best nature hikes in the La Platas. An explosion of ladybugs once covered the summit. Horney toads press their bellies against

Strange and beautiful spotted coral root thrives in the high woodlands along the route.

warming rocks. Fresh bear and elk scat is an indication of the company you'll be keeping. Among the winged creatures, watch for swallowtail butterfly, Milbert's tortoiseshell butterfly, red-tailed hawk, and golden eagles.

An unusual array of flowers may be found on this relatively low elevation hike. A partial list includes: the rare Pagosa bladderpod, Rocky Mountain milkvetch, pygmy bitterroot, sugarbowl, evening primrose, dogwood, clematis, blue-eyed Mary, townsendia, wild iris, sweet cicely, New Mexican senecio, Rocky Mountain and toadflax penstemon, golden smoke, mule's ear, green gentian, scarlet beeblossom, and spotted coralroot.

MOUNTAINEERS

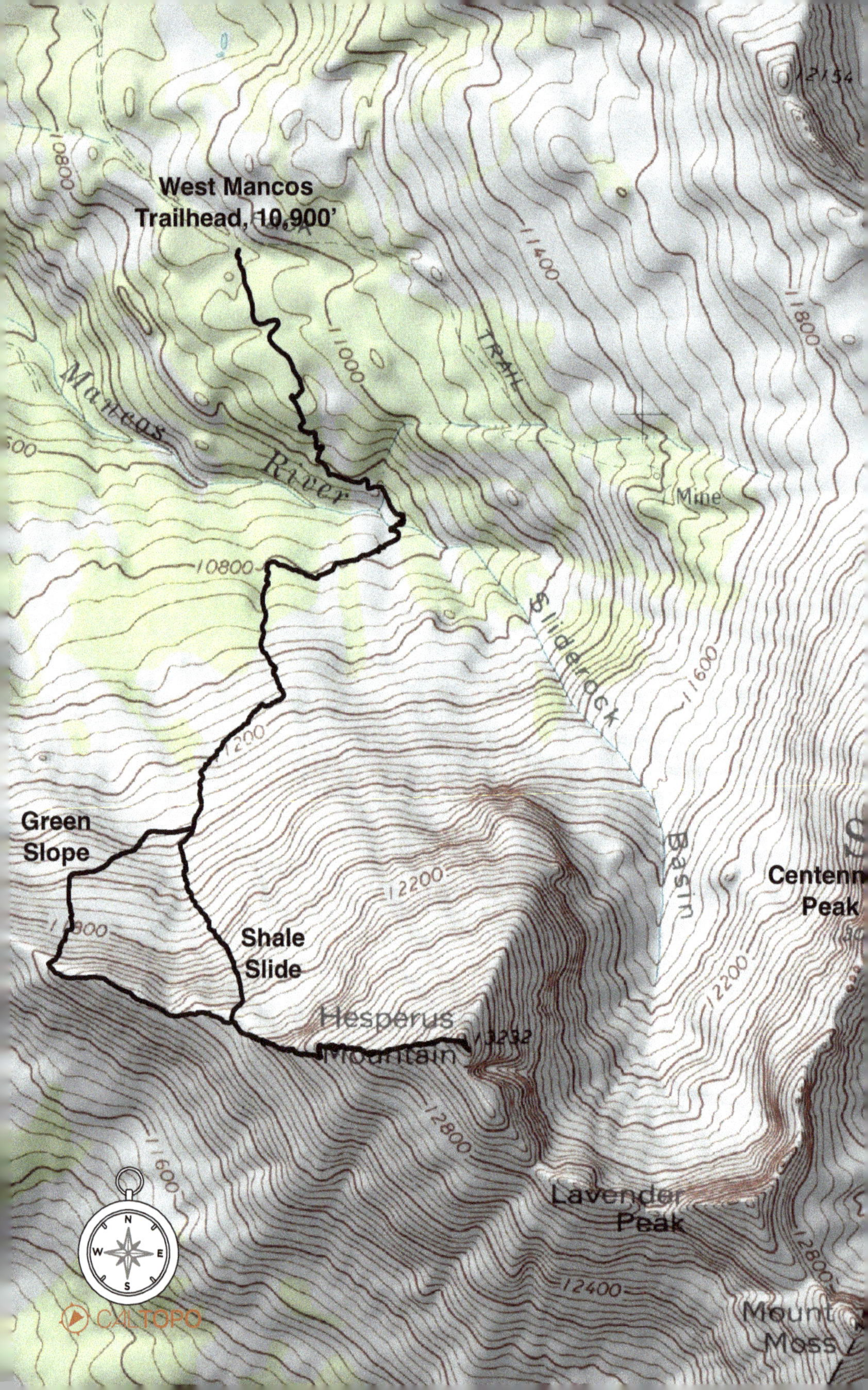

West Mancos
Trailhead, 10,900'
Mancos River
TRAIL
Mine
10800
11400
11000
11800
11600
12200
Sliderock
Basin
Green
Slope
11900
12200
Shale
Slide
Hesperus
Mountain
13232
12800
Centenm
Peak
Lavender
Peak
11600
12400
12800
Mount
Moss
12154
N
W   E
S
CALTOPO

HESPERUS MOUNTAIN, 13,238'

Dibé Ntsaa, "Sheep Mountain," is the mountain First Man and First Woman created for the north. They made it firm to the earth with a rainbow and adorned it with beads of jet black, with plants of many varieties.
— Trebbe Johnson

Hesperus Mountain marks the northern boundary of the traditional homeland of the Navajo. It is the Sacred Mountain of the North. The eastern cardinal point is Sierra Blanca Peak in the Sangre de Cristo Range; in the south it is Mount Taylor in New Mexico; and in the west, Humphreys Peak near Flagstaff, Arizona. Hesperus is the highest eminence in the La Plata Range with a rise of 2,844 feet. It is one of the most difficult peaks to navigate with multiple route options from both north and south. The standard route from the north is described with one variation. The upper mountain is climbed by way of the west ridge. Ascend a stair-step progression of cliff-slope formations, staying on the ridge to the summit.

ABOUT THIS HIKE
Distance: 5.2 miles
Elevation Gain: 2,700 feet
Total Time: 5:00 to 6:30
Route Surface: trail, primarily off-trail, scree and talus blocks
Class: 3
Exposure: mild
Navigation: challenging

Travel

Measure distance from the intersection of US 160 and CO 184 in Mancos. At the signal, turn north toward Dolores. In 0.3 mile, at the sign for Mancos State Park, turn right on Montezuma CR 42. At 5.5 miles, the road becomes FSR 561, West Mancos Road. Pass the Transfer Campground at 10.3 miles where pavement ends. Stay on FSR 561 at 11.1 miles. Pass the Aspen Guard Station at 11.9 miles. Turn right at mile 12.4 on FSR 350, Spruce Mill Road. It remains smooth and graded until mile 18.8. Turn on the right spur signed for the Twin Lakes and Sharkstooth trailheads, FSR 346. The next 1.5 miles require 4WD, good

clearance, and sturdy tires. The track is rocky with potholes. There is dispersed camping along the road with ponds and a terrific view of Hesperus Mountain. The West Mancos Trailhead is 20.3 miles from Mancos. The small parking area holds six vehicles.

Route

Two trails take off from the parking lot at elevation 10,900 feet. The more frequently traveled Sharkstooth Trail bears east. Head south on the West Mancos Trail toward Transfer Campground. The north face of banded Hesperus Mountain beckons in clear view. Walk across a bucolic, flower-filled, tree-rimmed meadow and descend gradually through a climax forest.

In half a mile, cross the creek scurrying from the Sharkstooth–Centennial saddle. Soon after, span the Sliderock Basin drainage on a sturdy, five-log bridge. The streams join below the trail to become the North Fork of the West Mancos River. The path swings southwest and plows through native honeysuckle and then a delphinium stand seven feet high in a good flower year.

Arrowleaf senecio and mountain bluebells compete for sun in this flower fantasyland.

The green ramp just left of center at the ridgeline, beyond the line of trees, is your goal.

Take special note of a twin spruce portal at 0.85 mile. Continue on the West Mancos Trail for 0.1 mile past the portal as it goes slightly downhill. The social trail up Hesperus begins at a cluster of large, fallen trees that have been cleared from the trail, elevation 10,800 feet. The south-bearing path is clear at the turnoff but almost obliterated by flora and fallen timber in places farther on. The route takes advantage of a shallow gully and emerges from the woods on the east side of a small talus field. Cairns lead the way to a stand of conifers on a knoll at 1.2 miles, 11,160 feet.

From the treed knoll, follow the cairned route southwest across a slope of broken rock, willows, and tundra to elevation 11,400. The green slope ascent route and the shale slide descent route diverge here. Climbing the shale slide directly will shave 0.3 mile but it is laborious scaling the soft, coal-like granules. For the green slope approach, go west crossing below a green-topped moraine. Climb southwest, tracking between the runout of a rock glacier and the uphill edge of the willow line. Continue until you have a clear shot of the green slope going all the way to the ridge.

Pitch south, steeply up a thin strip of grass. Trekking poles are helpful. Arrive on the west ridge east of Point 11,891' at 1.9 miles, 12,040 feet. Turn east staying on the ridgetop. Mid-summer, the ridge is covered in blinding

In spite of its appearance, a route directly up this ridge-line is the safest way, and also the most fun. snow-like patches of phlox. Its wafting perfume induces alpine euphoria.

The approach concludes at 12,300 feet, 2.2 miles. Notice an unmaintained trail that leaves the ridge and makes for the south side of the mountain. The trail seeks to avoid some of the larger cliff bands but exacts a price before rejoining the ridge proper at 13,000 feet. The steep, exposed, and braided side-hill track alternates between soft, unstable shale, and slippery, resistant soil.

The following description, therefore, leads the climber directly up the spine. Most handsome Hesperus becomes your guide. The summit climb is 932 vertical feet over half a mile and takes roughly 45 minutes. The ascent looks imposing but this is the best segment of the journey for big-block scramblers.

Begin climbing left of the initial dark outcrop. Experience the alternating cliff-slope structure of the mountain while walking up through Mancos Shale to the base of the next cliff band. Hesperus is part of the La Plata Mountain laccolith which is an intrusion of magma between sedimentary

Right: A short wall provides some optional fun scrambling, but beware of fragile holds.

layers. Sediments in close contact with the magma were baked to recrystallized hornfels. The dark and light bands of rock so prevalent on Hesperus and Centennial are alternating layers of congealed magma (light bands) and baked sediment (dark bands).

The second cliff tier presents a Class 3 scramble on good rock. Some slabs are not well anchored so test all holds. This crux is the only pitch with exposure. It may be bypassed safely 100 feet to the south on a rudimentary trail that punches up the short wall.

Hold to the ridgeline while staying sufficiently away from the continuous, precipitous north edge. Surmount the rising stone staircase all the way to the crest. The mountain rounds off to reward those whose perseverance and desire propel them past the many obstacles to the summit at 2.7 miles. Hesperus Mountain is the heartbeat of the La Plata Range. Standing on the small apex, it is not a stretch to imagine the mountain pulsating beneath your feet.

From the highest point in the La Plata Mountains the field of vision is compelling and commanding. Close by, Centennial Peak is the red-banded mountain across Sliderock Basin to the east. Hesperus looks out over the most severe, ragged, and demanding peaks in the range. Skilled climbers

have reportedly traversed the technical ridge from Centennial to Lavender Peak. The Lavender to Hesperus segment is exposed Class 4. In the neighborhood to the south, the infamous Knife slices between West Babcock and Spiller peaks.

Lone Cone stands watch in the northwest. In the southwest lies Mesa Verde and Sleeping Ute Mountain. On a clear day, you can see beyond the curve of the world into Utah, New Mexico, and even Arizona. Hesperus predominates in stature and eternal significance. The mountain deserves our respect as the cardinal point of the North.

For the return, downclimb through the cliffrock as you came. The shale slide offers the easiest, quickest, and most thrilling descent. It is located just east of a patch of orange rock at 12,280 feet. Divert from the ridge to the north.

Lose 500 feet effortlessly in just a few minutes. The way is bejeweled by a range of columbine. There have never been so many state flowers in one location. At the bottom of the glissade, follow a trail to the green-topped moraine and track down the east side. Watch for cairns leading back to the treed knoll. A large rock stack typically marks the head of the gully route back to the West Mancos Trail. Turn right and re-cross the headwater streams of the Mancos River. A 200-foot hill-climb takes you back to the trailhead.

Climbing Hesperus is so deeply satisfying. The mountain has sufficient power to be grounded right where it is and to be carried around in our hearts to inform our days.

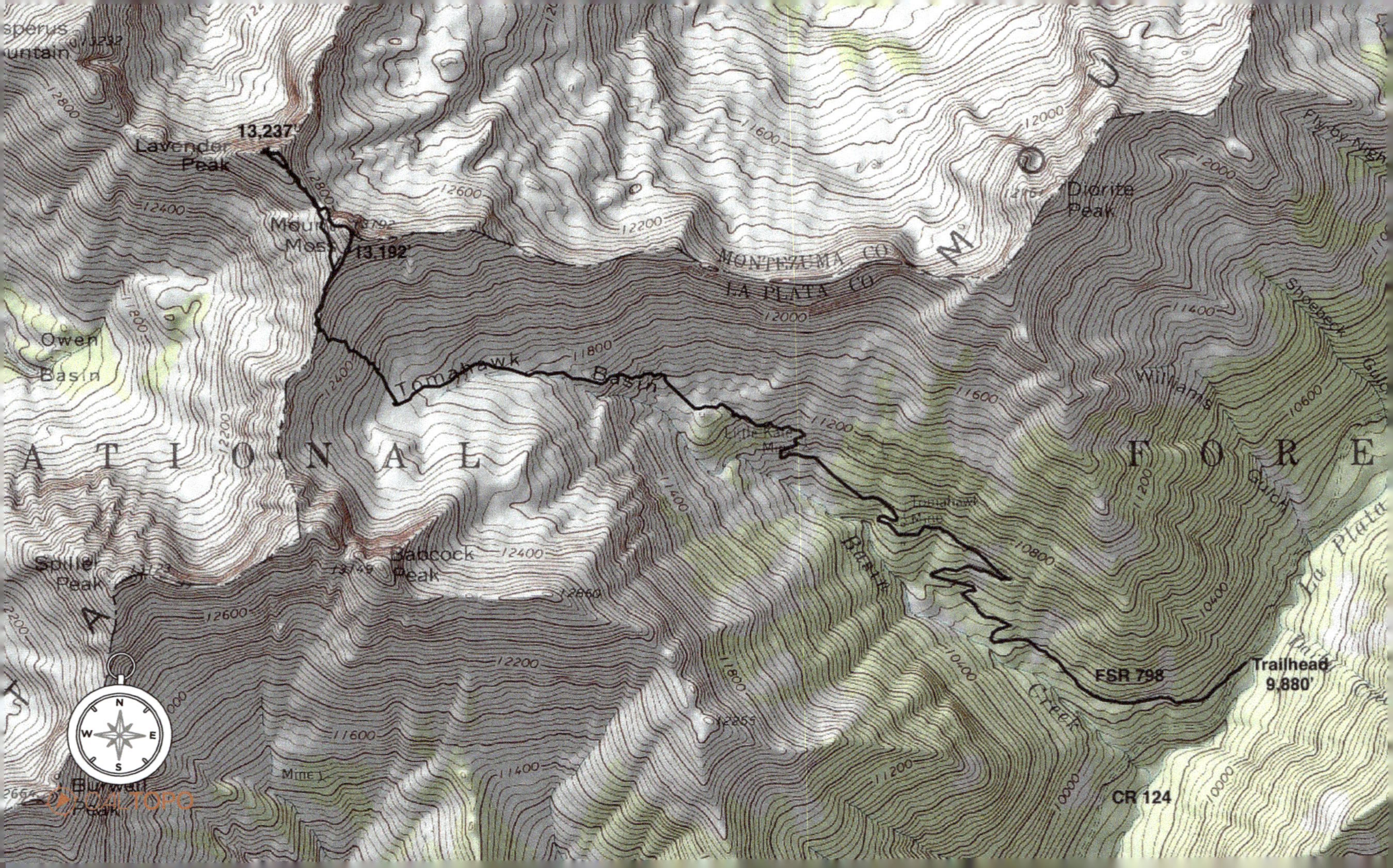

sperus Mountain
Lavender Peak
13,237
Mount Moss
13,192
Owen Basin
Spiller Peak
Burwell Peak
N A T I O N A L
MONTEZUMA CO
LA PLATA CO
M O U
Diorite Peak
Pixby Nigh
Tomahawk Basin
Babcock Peak
Little Kate M
Tomahawk Mine
Williams
Shoesock Gulch
F O R E
La Plata
Mine 1
Creek
FSR 798
Trailhead 9,880'
CR 124
CALTOPO

MOUNT MOSS, 13,192'
AND LAVENDER PEAK, 13,237'

Life is either a daring adventure or nothing at all.

— Helen Keller

Venture through Tomahawk Basin to the triangulated magnificence of Mount Moss and the mythical towers of Lavender Peak. From the West Tower there are transcendent views of neighboring Hesperus Mountain and Centennial Peak, and the vast reaches of the Colorado Plateau. This demanding, off-trail, exposed climb is suitable for proven scramblers. This is the authors' favorite hike in the La Platas.

ABOUT THIS HIKE
Distance: 8 miles
Elevation Gain: 3,800 feet
Time: 6:30 to 8:00
Route Surface: jeep track, off-trail, steep slopes, giant talus
Class: 3+
Exposure: considerable
Navigation: challenging

Travel

Measure distance from the junction of US 160 and La Plata Canyon Road, CR 124. After passing the hamlet of Mayday the road turns to smooth dirt at 4.6 miles. In 8.5 miles the roadbed deteriorates with sharp, sizable rocks. A 2WD vehicle with good tires and moderate clearance should suffice. Parking is limited alongside the road at 10.6 miles. The hike goes west up Forest Service Road 798 into Tomahawk Basin. With high clearance, 4WD low, and considerable moxie and skill, it is possible to drive up the steep and rocky technical two-track 1.9 miles to Little Kate Mine.

Route

From the trailhead in La Plata Canyon at 9,880 feet, walk westerly through an aspen forest interspersed with talus flows. In autumn the golden passage

is among the finest in the La Platas. The old wagon road tracks above perennial Basin Creek to a split at one mile in lower Tomahawk Basin. Stay on the main road as it hooks east on a long traverse before returning west to come alongside the Tomahawk stamp mill.

The mill was constructed by the Tomahawk Mining Company in 1904. Exploratory work was done on promising veins in diorite stock. Recovery of precious metals was poor and mining operations in Tomahawk Basin concluded in 1911. Clamber down below the mill to examine intact wooden wheels, steel grates, and massive timbers.

At 1.9 miles, elevation 10,920 feet, leave the wagon road as it makes a sharp switchback to the east at the Little Kate Mine. Continuing west, a stairstep series of steep pitches and shallow climbs must be negotiated to reach upper Tomahawk Basin. Commanding Mount Moss, composed of white-gray stone, rises north of the headwall. The following instructions will help you find the way. If they seem confusing, simply stay north of Basin Creek and let the landscape be your guide.

The exit from the upper basin can be found on the ridge directly above the hiker's head in this photo. Take advantage of grass slopes to ease your climb.

Left: The distinctive three towers of Lavender Peak rise above the precipitous ridge from Mount Moss.

Follow a social trail up a steep hillside to a bench, staying well right of a prominent rock outcrop. At the next level, the footpath utilizes the bed of an historic, steel pipeline. Next, bypass a waterfall on the right. A faint trail climbs right of a deep-gray outcrop before turning left through a short stand of willows. You will then go by a couple of outlier black boulders. Locate a long-abandoned mining road adjacent to Basin Creek. The rocky track is particularly useful crossing a large talus field. The gently rising basin butts up against a highly angled slope at the base of the south ridge of Mount Moss at 12,100 feet.

An impregnable section of ridge flows south from Mount Moss before it is splintered by weaknesses. While you may contact the ridge in several locations, it is easiest to climb the steep, grassy slopes as far to the right as possible—just south of the upper scree field. With a little luck, you will locate a wildcat trail, a golden path up the final 100 feet to the ridgetop.

Upon reaching the ridge at about 12,720 feet, turn north. Almost immediately bypass a vertical wall on its west side. After about 100 yards of

traversing on good, trustworthy rock, return to the spine. Scramble on angular blocks to the summit at 3.7 miles.

The pyramidal crest is cloaked with stately boulders standing guard over the wildest terrain in the range. Mount Moss is one of five La Plata thirteeners, all visible from this vantage point. Hesperus Mountain and Lavender Peak are a stone's throw to the northwest. One mile north is Centennial Peak. Looking back on the climbing route, the south ridge of Mount Moss terminates at West Babcock Peak. Of the three Babcocks, only Middle Babcock (13,161 feet) is a ranked summit. The La Plata Knife is the sharp, serrated slice of stone spanning to Spiller Peak. Diorite Peak is two miles east beyond a dangerous, impassible ridge.

If you are tapped or the south ridge of Mount Moss tested your mettle, this is your turnaround summit. Class 3+ scrambling with exposure is required to surmount the three towers of Lavender Peak. The saving grace is solid rock with good holds making for a superlative adventure.

From Mount Moss, descend northwest on well-seated talus to the saddle

Cresting the East Tower on excellent rock, it is easy to believe your journey is at an end, but the magic continues.

at 12,880 feet. As you begin the Lavender ascent, the side walls of vertical couloirs encapsulate banded Centennial Peak.

Cross a stable, thin ridge to the East Tower of Lavender Peak. Welcome to the castle maze where precise navigation is imperative. Face the rock for the challenging and spirited downclimb. Some climbers will need a spot. This tower may be flanked on the south but any ridge bypass has inherent risks.

Drop into the wedge between the East and Middle towers. Traverse west laterally around the base of Middle Tower. The passage shows signs of use but there are no cairns on this route. Scale dependable boulders, using four-point climbing to reach the diminutive saddle between Middle and West towers.

Finish on the exhilarating West Tower where you will find the peak register. The zenith is essentially one block of stone with room for three climbers. Be sure to climb Middle Tower as well.

The exact height of Lavender Peak is unknown and subject to on-going speculation. The elevation of nearby Hesperus Mountain has also come into

question, however in all recent iterations of re-measurement, Hesperus has remained the highest prominence in the La Plata range.

For the return, downclimb into the notch between West and Middle towers. Then, head east, cutting just south of East Tower. Upon arriving at the Lavender-Moss saddle, contour below Mount Moss to regain the south ridge.

Perhaps only a foot shorter than mighty Hesperus, the single-block summit of Lavender is without doubt the emotional high-point of the range.

At the now familiar insurmountable gendarme, bypass west and once back on the ridge look immediately for your descent route into Tomahawk Basin. The faint use trail is obliterated by tundra 100 feet below the ridge.

Watch for soaring bald and golden eagles, and playful, chortling ravens in the upper basin.

Diorite Peak
Mount Moss
MONTEZUMA CO
LA PLATA CO
M
TIONAL
FOR
Tomahawk Basin
Williams
Little Kate Mine
Tomahawk Mine
East Babcock Peak
13,149
Fuller Peak
Burwell Peak
Mine
FSR 798
Trailhead
9,880
CR 124
CREEK
×2255
12,400
12,600
12,200
11,400
11,800
11,600
11,200
11,400
12,000
12,200
12,600
11,600
12,000
11,400
11,600
12,400
10,800
10,400
10,400
10,000
10,000
11,200
11,800
CALTOPO

EAST BABCOCK PEAK, 13,149'

My soul can find no staircase to Heaven unless it be through Earth's loveliness.
— Michelangelo

While East Babcock is not the highest of the three Babcock peaks—that honor belongs to Middle Babcock—it is the only summit with a designated elevation on the La Plata topographical map. Access the climb through Tomahawk Basin where beauty is startling, big, and bright. Adrenalized Class 3 scrambling scales the ultra-thin, razorback east ridge to an isolated crest with mind-numbing, heart-wrenching views of nearby peaks. Ascending East Babcock is an annual sojourn for some La Plata aficionados.

ABOUT THIS HIKE
Distance: 7.6 miles
Elevation Gain: 3,300 feet
Time: 5:30 to 7:30
Route Surface: jeep track, social trail, off-trail, talus
Class: 3
Exposure: considerable
Navigation: challenging

Travel

Measure distance from the junction of US 160 and La Plata Canyon Road, CR 124. After passing the hamlet of Mayday the road turns to smooth dirt at 4.6 miles. In 8.5 miles the roadbed deteriorates with sharp, sizable rocks. A 2WD vehicle with good tires and moderate clearance should suffice. Parking is limited alongside the road at 10.6 miles. The hike goes west up Forest Service Road 798.

Route

The route into upper Tomahawk Basin reprises the trek to Mount Moss and Lavender Peak. In brief, from the junction of La Plata Canyon Road and FSR 798, elevation 9,880 feet, walk westerly up the historic wagon road as it tracks above Basin Creek. Upon reaching the lower basin, the road splits at one mile. Follow the main track as it cranks east on a long traverse before switching

back west to pass the Tomahawk stamp mill.

While it is indeed possible to punch up to the east ridge of East Babcock from the lower basin it is a miserable, high-angled proposition. Therefore, remain on the road to the Little Kate Mine at 1.9 miles, elevation 10,920 feet. Navigating a series of stairstep pitches and shallow climbs over the next mile into upper Tomahawk is tricky. However, fragments of social trail assist. Remember to stay on the north side of the watercourse.

Follow a braided social trail northwest up a steep, slippery slope to a bench, staying well right of a beige outcrop. The path moderates on the bed of a defunct steel pipeline. Bypass the waterfall in the center of the basin by climbing to the right of a gray outcrop. The faint trail then bears left to plow through a stand of willows.

Pass a couple of black boulders seated on the next terrace. The climbing ameliorates and the track moves closer to the creek, all the while bearing west into the basin. A long-abandoned mining road is particularly useful for crossing a large block field.

As you rise to greater heights, acquaint yourself with the five mountains rimming the Tomahawk bowl. Diorite Peak is just off the northeast wall; Mount Moss is in the northwest corner; and the imposing north faces of West, Middle, and East Babcock peaks are on the south divide between the Tomahawk and Boren basins. The gendarme-splintered arête spanning

the bowl is openly inhospitable to the climber.

When the slope levels out in the upper basin, angle over to the creek. Where you cross the streamway is not critical; do so somewhere between 11,800 and 12,000 feet. The next objective is the saddle between Point 12,860' and East Babcock. There is no single best path initially. Zigzag south on ramps of tundra, threading between blocks. Here, one gets the exhilarating impression this mountain really wants to be climbed. Reach a flat reprieve at 12,260 feet.

Round to the east of the peak's northeast ridge where the saddle comes into view. Work up the large and rickety talus field. The rock is bigger and more accepting near the base of the ridge. About 300 feet off the saddle there is a remarkable stone shelf, rather like a road, that leads southeast onto a social trail. The essential footpath makes a rising traverse across a scree field and hits the saddle west of Point 12,860' at 3.55 miles, elevation 12,740 feet.

From the saddle, it is 409 feet of vertical over a quarter mile on a knife-edge to the summit. The entire spine is the crux of this hike. This segment of the trek is for proven Class 3 scramblers experienced with foot-wide passages and serious exposure. A fall could be catastrophic.

For those who continue on, East Babcock provides a rare and ideal climb. For one may follow a direct line to the summit without even once deviating from the ridgetop. Likewise, do not deviate from undivided concentration. There is an abundance of solid rock. And while holds are

East Babcock forms one shoulder (left-center) of the tour-de-force southern wall of upper Tomahawk Basin.

generally good, test them all. For the experienced mountaineer, the thin but accommodating east ridge is the definition of happiness.

Alight on the softly rounded, roomy-enough apex at 3.8 miles. Of the summits in the La Plata Mountains, the Babcock peaks and Spiller Peak down the way are among the most challenging—lusty, wild tangles of shattered rock. Looking west, across the no-access abyss is Middle Babcock Peak. To the northwest is Mount Moss, a Tomahawk companion, followed by Lavender Peak and Hesperus Mountain, only one-and-a-half miles away.

Tucked into the earth are brilliant splashes of alpine wildflowers. Look for purple fringe and sky pilot competing for the most colorful award. There are little pink mats of moss campion and white alp lily on a single delicate stem. The flowers, so soft and ephemeral contrast with the eternal stone staircase that lifted you to this mountaintop.

MIDDLE
BABCOCK PEAK, 13,161'

*So, if you cannot understand that there is something in man which
responds to the challenge of this mountain and goes out to meet it,
that the struggle is the struggle of life itself upward and forever upward,
then you won't see why we go. What we get from this adventure
is just sheer joy. And joy is, after all, the end of life.
We do not live to eat and make money.*

— George Leigh Mallory

The three steeply-pitched Babcock peaks are separated by deep, impassible crevices. Although they are tightly packed, each presents wildly different challenges for the climber. Middle Babcock, the tallest of the three and the only ranked summit, is accessed from Boren Creek Basin. Begin on a lengthy, cobbly track. Pitch up a rubble slope into the confines of a couloir with large, unstable material. Alight on the balancing point between the Boren and Tomahawk basins. The approach over, finish with a Class 3+ fantastical scramble on good rock with serious exposure. This is a classic La Plata Mountains climb for experienced mountaineers in groups of two or three.

ABOUT THIS HIKE
Distance: 7.3 miles
Elevation Gain: 3,950 feet
Time: 5:30 to 8:00
Route Surface: jeep track, steep and unstable slopes, helmets recommended
Class: 3+
Exposure: serious
Navigation: challenging

Travel

Measure distance from the junction of US 160 and La Plata Canyon Road, CR 124. After passing the hamlet of Mayday, the road turns to smooth dirt at 4.6 miles. Park in a pullout at 8.1 miles, just past Boren Creek.

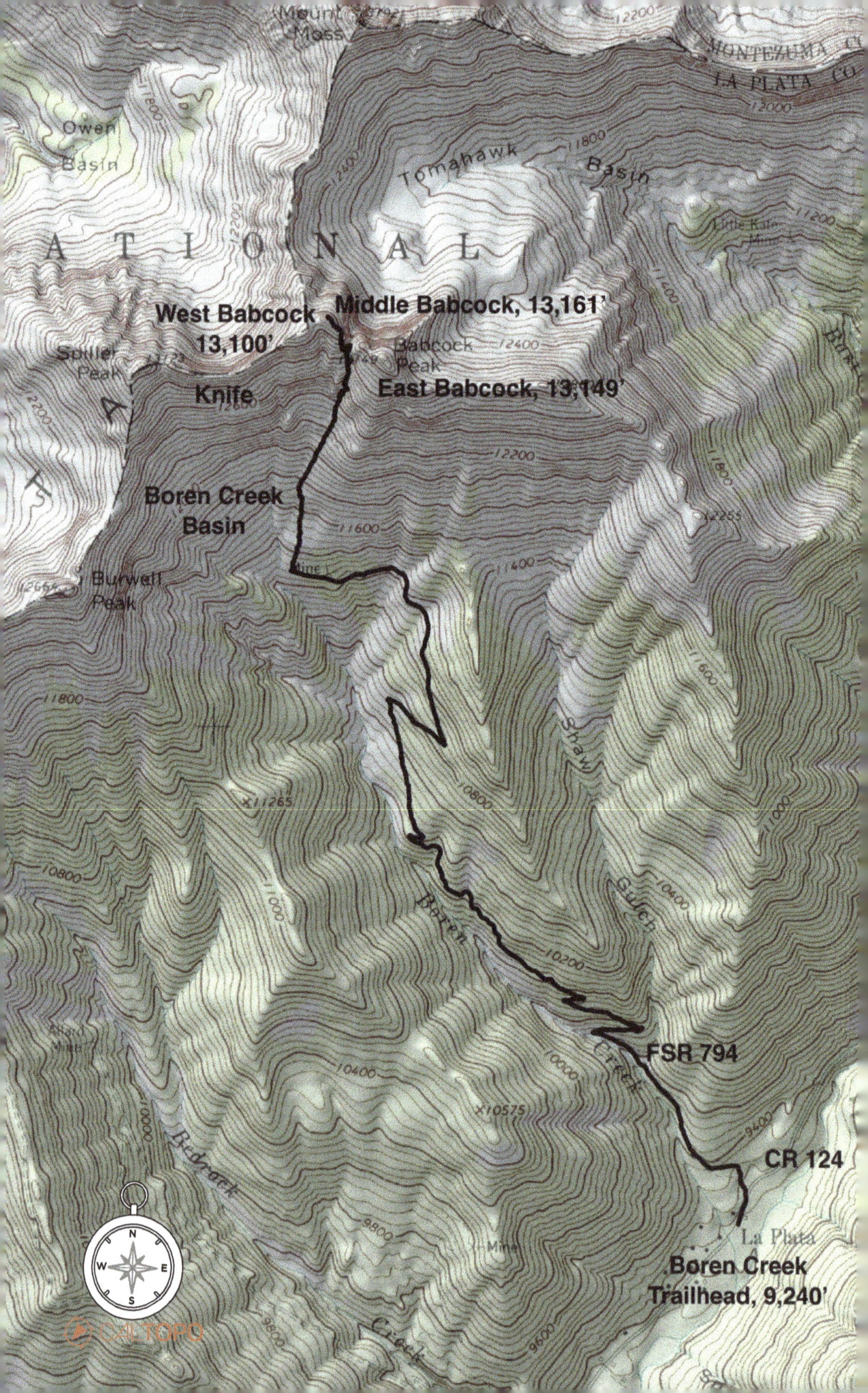

Owen Basin
Spiller Peak
A T I O N A L
West Babcock 13,100'
Middle Babcock, 13,161'
Babcock Peak
East Babcock, 13,149'
Knife
Boren Creek Basin
Burwell Peak
Tomahawk Basin
La Plata Co
MONTEZUMA Co
Shaw Gulch
Boren Creek
FSR 794
CR 124
La Plata
Boren Creek Trailhead, 9,240'
N
S
E
W
CALTOPO

Route

From the parking pullout, elevation 9,240 feet, walk up La Plata Canyon Road about 200 feet and head northwest up Boren Creek Road, FSR 794. The rough and rocky footbed is ameliorated by the riffling creek to the south, shimmering aspen, and lush wildflower-infused hillsides. Cross Shaw Gulch at 0.5 mile. At 1.7 miles, 10,480 feet, the route to Burwell Peak branches left. Stay on the main track, deeply shaded by Colorado blue spruce.

The route to Middle Babcock leaves the Boren Creek Road at 2.8 miles, 11,300 feet. Pause and take a moment to locate the proper route. Five mountains encircle high-angle Boren Basin. Burwell Peak is the highpoint on the southwest pivot. From there, the rim points north to Spiller Peak and then it swings east. The peaks on the precipitous north wall of the basin run in quick succession. To the right of Spiller is the crux of the Knife at the "tooth." Next, is the south wall of the Knife, West Babcock with the smooth stone swale, Middle Babcock, our climbing couloir, and East Babcock. To confuse the matter, the La Plata quad labels East Babcock as Babcock Peak, 13,149'. And yet, Middle Babcock is the highest of the trio at 13,161 feet. It is the only ranked summit on the entire span.

The off-trail segment mounts 1,880 feet in less than 0.9 mile. To get started, hike north through the krummholz, staying on the turf as best you

Middle Babcock's daunting ramparts rise above a massive field of its own debris (center).

Occasional but unreliable holds can be found on the west wall of the extremely steep and unstable couloir.

can. The initial climb is arduous, even tedious on a combination of grass, scree, talus, and boulders. At 12,000 feet, the pitch steepens and talus rolls out from underfoot.

Note of Caution: We once witnessed two three-foot cubes of stone cut loose from a Babcock couloir and, gathering more boulders, bounce-fly at 100 mph down the center of the basin where we had been moments prior. They skidded to a halt just shy of the jeep track. It was a narrow and lucky miss. Please be fully aware that your presence in the basin is potentially dangerous.

Enter through the gates of the Middle Babcock couloir at elevation 12,460 feet. Boulders in the chute are abraded and easily activated. Climb in lock-step with your partner. The west wall has better grip than the east; make use of its secure holds. The passageway curves left and keeps on going.

Right: Looking back at the top of the couloir, this short section must be traversed with delicacy.

The summit ridge rises almost vertically at first, but the superior rock provides relief.

The couloir ends at 12,900 feet, 3.5 miles, the intimate tipping point between two major basins in the La Plata Mountains. The southeast ridge of Middle Babcock hurtles down and terminates in the constricted cleft. The cliff-framed vista restricts the field of vision to a slim, solitary tower and a narrow gash plummeting into Tomahawk Basin.

The summit is 0.15 mile afar. For experienced scramblers, the journey from here is pure pleasure. However, hikers with a fear of heights should turn back now. To access the southeast climbing ridge, pitch up the ramp, visible a few feet to the southwest.

The ensuing Class 3+ terrain is steepest for 120 feet above the ramp. Most holds are good and solid but test them all the way to the summit. The route is not cairned; make mental notes of your approach so you don't overshoot the ramp on the downclimb.

The grade softens and the razorback constricts. Stay right on the ridgecrest unless forced off momentarily. The crux initiates at two stone pillars. One of us has climbed the mountain numerous times and has tried different tactics at the crux. First, hug your way around the pillars. Then, either stay right on the spiked spine or maneuver slightly off-ridge on the north. Friends have stepped down to the south before the pillars for a longer bypass. All choices are seriously exposed and some would argue a move or two is Class 4. Return to the ridgetop at first opportunity.

Polish off the climb on a narrow reef of rock and arrive on the compact crest at 3.65 miles.

Middle Babcock is tucked into a compressed landscape. East Babcock Peak is roughly 0.1 mile away. West Babcock is but a stone's throw across

The awkward center of this last spiky section is probably the safest.

a fearsome gap. Spiller Peak is on the far side of the Knife at the west end of the ridgeline.

Middle Babcock is amongst the community of wild heights. The five ranked La Plata thirteeners are all positioned in the northern tier of the West Block. They include banded Hesperus Mountain, the three towers of Lavender Peak (eclipsing Centennial Peak from this vantage point), and the northwest cornerstone of Tomahawk Basin, Mount Moss.

The downclimb from the peak to the road typically takes as much time and effort as the ascent. Maneuver down the southeast scramble aiming for the ramp, the unavoidable slick slide into the couloir.

Hold your concentration in spite of any physical fatigue or mental monotony. Tenuously balanced boulders cut loose at the slightest touch. If the weather holds, be sure to visit the distinctive orange outcrop a good ways down toward the road. Walk out the top line of stone and balance on the miniature pedestal. Watch for eagles and peregrine falcons in the upper basin.

Mount Moss
Jackson Fork
West
Mancos River
Owen Basin
JEEP TRAIL
Ridge
N A T I O N
West Babcock
Pt. 12,201'
Lake 11,840'
Spiller Peak
13,123'
The Knife
Park 10,800'
Slide Path
Bench Trail
Rush Basin
Saddle 12,500'
Prospect
Mine
Boren Basin
Mine
Burwell Peak
CALTOPO

SPILLER PEAK, 13,123'

Attention is the beginning of devotion.

— Mary Oliver

Three prominent ridges radiate from Spiller, all of them troublesome for the climber. Three basins surround the mountain but only two offer approach. The route to the Burwell-Spiller saddle from the west is more direct and easier than the tedious trek through Boren Basin. Rock on the required south ridge is fractured and friable, holds are unreliable, and exposure is serious. However, this route is considerably less dangerous than traversing the east ridge over The Knife.

ABOUT THIS HIKE

Distance: 5.2 miles
Elevation Gain: 2,700 feet
Time: 4:30 to 6:00
Route Surface: off-trail, steep, rotten rock
Class: 3 on south ridge
Exposure: considerable
Navigation: moderate

Travel

From the US 550/160 intersection in Durango, travel west on US 160 for 24.7 miles to the signed Echo Basin Road and turn north. Measure distance from here. Stay on the main road, passing old homesteads and hay meadows. In 2.4 miles, continue straight on FSR 566 when the road turns to gravel. The road deteriorates at 3.8 miles where winter plowing stops. The track climbs steadily through scrub oak to a cattle guard at 6.4 miles. Directly east is The Hogback. Beyond the guard are literally acres of blooming mule's ears in early summer. At 6.8 miles, bear right at the fork, staying on FSR 566. Climbing, the road passes through an aspen forest. At 8.0 miles, the road forks again; stay left. (A right turn will get you there but the road is much worse.) At 9.9 miles, go right. High clearance and good tires are necessary on the rocky track. At 11.6 miles, turn right; left is 566G. Pass a large meadow with a beautiful view of Helmet Peak. At 13.6 miles, go left onto 566H. Park in a small clearing at 14.6 miles or venture another 0.2 mile and park near a tiny pond.

Route

From the parking pullout at 10,800 feet, continue up the road for 0.25 mile to the base of an avalanche path. The pitch is direct and steep. The climb may be softened on a network of abandoned roads but that adds considerable distance. At 11,200 feet, veer south on an old mining road if you would like to visit a prospect. Watch for golden eagles circling above the ridge crest.

In just 0.8 mile, gain the ridge between Helmet Peak and Point 12,201' at 11,900 feet. Crest Point 12,201', continue east along the ridge, and drop to

The peak makes its first appearance with fresh snow under a crisp October sky.

the Spiller saddle at 11,940 feet. Brilliant rock contrasts with a cerulean sky.

Reach the shore of the tundra-bound lake in Rush Basin, headwaters of the East Mancos River, at 11,840 feet, 1.7 miles. Scope a route to the Spiller-Burwell saddle. A subtle bench and historic trail fragments offer slim help. Resist the temptation to climb the west ridge as it is riddled with serious obstacles.

Skittering across chunky talus requires patience. However, the slope is considerably more stable than the endlessly tedious scree field on the east-side approach through Boren Basin.

Crest the ridgeline in the vicinity of Saddle 12,500' at 2.2 miles. Look deep into La Plata Canyon and across to the eastern block of the La Plata range. From here it is 0.4 mile to the summit.

There is nothing especially tricky about this straightforward ridge ascent. Stay close to the centerline. However, passage is complicated by crumbly rock. Hand and footholds are undependable on Class 3 scrambles; test them all. Maintain steely attention. Be especially mindful when forced onto open slopes or confined inside chutes. I've been on this ridge repeatedly and it has garnered my respect.

The ridge suddenly opens to a vista of Hesperus Mountain, Lone Cone, and the fourteeners in the San Miguel Mountains.

The challenge eases as you approach the rocky crown. Spiller Peak is one of the more formidable peaks in the La Platas and summiting is incredibly satisfying. North are intimate views of Hesperus Mountain, the towers of Lavender Peak, and Mount Moss. Adjacent to the south is Burwell Peak.

The Knife traverses the east ridge of Spiller to West Babcock Peak. It is

one of Colorado's finest (and notorious) scrambles. It is highly advisable to begin the half-mile-long traverse from West Babcock so you can up-climb the near vertical crux.

Back in Rush Basin, you may return over Point 12,201' but then you will miss an enrapturing landscape feature, the irresistible tableland that resides between the out-going ridge and the river canyon well below. The routes are the same distance, 0.8 mile. The tundra-topped terrace carries the gentle stream flowing from the lake. A wildcat trail materializes nicely above a willow patch.

Pass above a weakness in the cliffs revealing the East Mancos River. At one time there were more active mines in this basin than anywhere else in the La Platas. The trail ascends about 100 feet to close the loop on the ridge near the top of the slide path.

LEWIS MOUNTAIN, 12,740'
AND SNOWSTORM PEAK, 12,511'

As the hand held before the eye conceals the greatest mountain, so the little earthly life hides from the glance the enormous lights and mysteries of which the world is full, and he who can draw it away from before his eyes, as one draws away a hand, beholds the great shining of the inner worlds.

— Rabbi Nachmann

The mystique of Lewis Mountain is simple. It is not what it appears. Viewed from Durango, the bastion looks robust, big-boned, and alluring. In reality, the mountain takes the shape of a loosely draped necklace. Strung along the thin thread are a dozen upthrusting prominences. The ridgecrest is narrow and exposed for a full three miles. There are several access points—this stem and loop begins in Columbus Basin and gains the ridge via an historic mining trail that ascends to a 12,180-foot pass. From there, Snowstorm Peak is a quick out-and-back. There are three segments of knife-edge between the pass and the Lewis Mountain summit. Because of the length and vertiginous nature of the razorback spine, this traverse is advisable for experienced and agile climbers only. Your dogs will thank you for leaving them at home.

ABOUT THIS HIKE
Distance: 5.8 miles
Elevation Gain: 3,000 feet
Time: 5:00 to 7:00
Route Surface: jeep track, old burro trail, primarily off-trail on variable rock
Class: 3
Exposure: serious
Navigation: challenging

Travel

In a 4WD vehicle with good clearance and sturdy tires, measure distance from the junction of US 160 and La Plata Canyon Road, CR 124. After passing the hamlet of Mayday the road turns to smooth dirt at 4.6 miles. In 8.5 miles the roadbed deteriorates. At 12.0 miles the road splits. Turn right on FSR 498, the track into Columbus Basin. The road is steep and the rocks are sharp. Drive for 0.9 mile and park in a wide pullout on the left. A distinctive fallen log cabin is on the right.

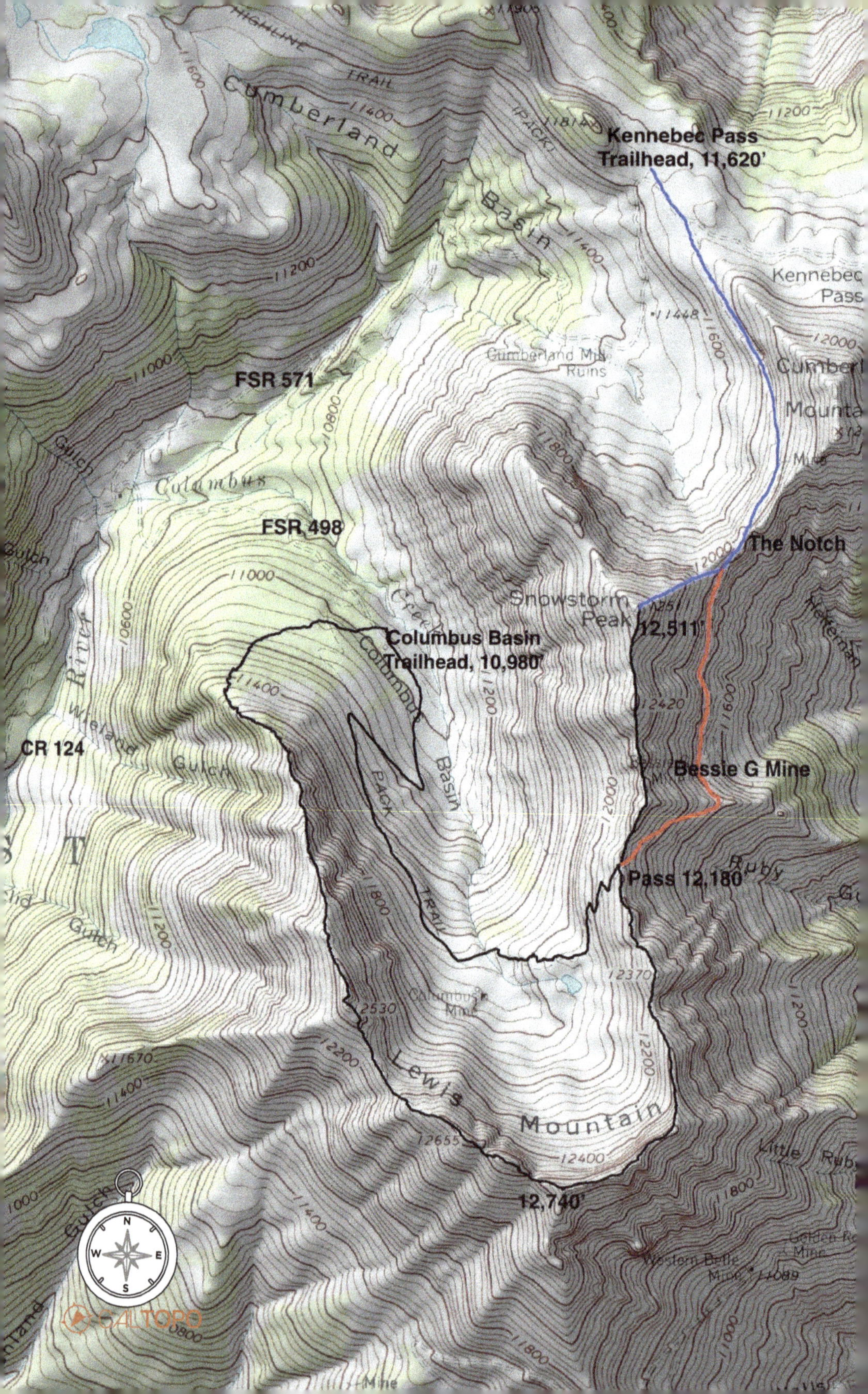

Kennebec Pass
Trailhead, 11,620'
Kennebec
Pass
Cumberland
Basin
HIGHLINE
TRAIL
PACK
11448
Cumberland Mine
Ruins
Cumberl
Mounta
Mine
512
FSR 571
Columbus
FSR 498
Creek
The Notch
Snowstorm
Peak
12,511'
Columbus Basin
Trailhead, 10,980'
Columbus
Basin
12420
11 600
Bessie G Mine
CR 124
Gulch
PACK
Pass 12,180'
Ruby
Gulch
12370
Columbus Mine
12530
Lewis
12200
11670
11400
Mountain
12655
12400
12,740'
Little
Ruby
Western Belle
Mine
11089
Golden R
Mine
1000
CALTOPO

Route

Scree slopes careen down the sweeping bowl rimmed by the mighty Snowstorm Peak and Lewis Mountain arc. Having made several approaches and iterations on the crestline, we consider the following route our favorite for its relative ease of passage. The basin is incised by old wagon roads that once served the Columbus Mine, Lucky Boy Tunnel, and Moonlight Prospect. A burro trail went over the pass to even more mines on the east side, including the Bessie G.

The first objective is the pass in the low saddle between the mountains. From the parking pullout in lower Columbus Basin, elevation 10,980 feet, walk south on FSR 498. The technical 4WD road gains elevation consistently and pleasantly. The major switchback at 0.3 mile might dissuade you but the track is an efficient route. You certainly could walk up through the center of the basin but it takes longer.

It is a little tricky transitioning to the pass trail and staying on it. The road swings east and at 1.2 miles, 11,680 feet, crosses Columbus Creek, the outlet of a small, headwater lake. A few paces past the stream, watch for a

cairn indicating the trail as it leaves from the right side of the road. The footpath wanders up a hill, marked periodically with large cairns. If you lose the path, look for it as you top the hill to the north of the lake.

Make sure you locate the indispensable old burro trail as it does a rising traverse to the north across a scree slope. Other headwall routes have been field tested and rejected as too steep. The miner's trail switchbacks up to the pass, cresting at 1.8 miles, elevation 12,180 feet.

Snowstorm Peak, 12,511'

The spur to Snowstorm is 1.2 miles roundtrip with 700 feet of climbing. The walk is pretty tame with just one short narrow stretch. There are six knobs on the rough rim. One rocky outcrop may be easily flanked near its crest on the east side. The "Red Ball," Point 12,420', is a false summit. Snowstorm is an excellent vantage point. The northeast ridge drops radically into The Notch at the head of Cumberland Basin. Flat-topped,

Successfully negotiating "The Blade" elicits a triumphant but anxious smile.

carmine Cumberland Mountain embraces Kennebec Pass. The San Juan Mountains flare out into the great beyond.

Lewis Mountain, 12,740'

It is one mile to the Lewis Mountain summit from the pass. The footing is a mix of tundra, scraggy bedrock, sharp-edged talus, chipped rock, and loose scree. While the ridge is free of showstopper gendarmes, there are a couple you may wish to bypass. Holds vary in dependability—test methodically.

To begin, a fragmentary wildcat trail has developed. Half a mile from the pass the first and longest section of knife-edge commences. If you are uncomfortable with what you see, turn back. "The Blade" is the first significant obstacle. Some people straddle the rock's spine. There is a micro-ledge on the west side with decent footing. Once, while on the work-around my hold pulled off the mountain, so use caution.

The second splintered serrate leads onto a crest at the apex of the arc. On the La Plata quad this prominence ranks equal with the summit. But when you get out there, the true zenith is clearly the one with a south ridge pitching down to Eagle Pass. The map does not identify or number the highpoint of Lewis Mountain so its exact height is unknown.

The third knife traverses a high-angle scree slope before integrating into the sizable rock-covered crown at 3.9 miles. The mountaintop is a full-circle vantage point. Look out over companion peaks, Durango, and Lake

Nighthorse. Indian Trail Ridge points to the greater San Juan Mountains: the San Miguel Mountains, Mount Sneffels Wilderness, and the Grenadier Range and Needle Mountains in the Weminuche Wilderness.

Return to Columbus Basin

Descending the northwest ridge, the sawtooth series accumulates 300 feet of elevation gain. While the challenge decreases, it remains airy and the rock is loose and chipped so don't let your guard down. First, climb the banded prominence with the broad, flat top. The ridge dives to make ready for the final steep, 230-foot push to Point 12,530'.

In mid-August, Arctic gentian blossom on the ridgecrest. Dainty dotted saxifrage grow in crevices between big, beautiful blocks on the last roller. Stay on the thin ridge as it enters the timber at 11,800 feet. While it is tempting to start the eastward plunge along here, there is a lot of cliff structure. (I found this out the hard way.)

The ridge broadens as it swings southwest. A social trail leaves the

ridge on the right making for a bench below. That works, or linger for the golden path. Start rolling off the spine at about 11,500 feet and bear north. Cross a big flat and then curve east on gentle, floriferous slopes all the way to the log cabin, closing the loop at your vehicle. Mid-summer, wade through Grey's angelica, monkshood, osha, corn husk lily, bluebell, American bistort, king's crown, arrowleaf senecio, orange sneeze-weed, little sunflower, rosy paintbrush, and columbine.

The final section of ridge plunges steeply toward the ideal exit point at the edge of the krummholz.

Snowstorm Peak and Lewis Mountain commingle to create the longest, continuous ridge hike in the La Plata range. There is a sense that the entire spine is the summit, from its thin beginning just above The Notch, swinging around in a great arc, gathering Snowstorm, encompassing Lewis Mountain, and refusing to terminate until it dissipates in the waters of the La Plata River. The traverse demands the traveler's unbroken mindfulness. Whittled sheer by time and the forces of erosion, the slender rim affords a new perspective on one's inner world and the great circle of the horizon.

Blue-Line Route: Kennebec Pass Trailhead to Snowstorm Peak

A shuttle is required for both routes leaving from the Kennebec Pass Trailhead, elevation 11,620 feet. This is a quick but not trivial approach to Snowstorm Peak, 1.5 miles south with roughly 1,000 feet of vertical. Walk southeast on an old mining road that carries occasional 4WD traffic. Curve under the west slopes of Cumberland Mountain and pass through The Notch at 12,000 feet. Continue on the track until you are past an initial, razor-topped ridge remnant. Initiate the pitched climb up the hardscrabble northeast ridge. Move a little east to get around some cliffs and return to the ridge. If this challenging approach does not appeal, take the Red-Line route to the Bessie G Mine.

Red-Line Route: Bessie G Mine to Pass 12,180'

From the Kennebec Pass Trailhead, it is about two miles with 950 feet of climbing to the pass. Walk through The Notch and continue on the degenerating track for another half mile. The road becomes a trail after passing the Bessie G. The footpath mounts an eastward ridge and then climbs through Ruby Gulch to the pass.

Lewis Mountain from Eagle Pass

If your objective is to simply summit Lewis Mountain, you may climb the south ridge from Eagle Pass. The approach is very steep on poor rock, culminating directly on the peak. Walk or drive three miles up CR 124A to the upper parking turn-around at elevation 11,360 feet. Refer to the Bald Knob chapter for driving details and instructions for hiking to Eagle Pass. Lewis Mountain is 1.1 miles with 1,400 feet of vertical from the parking area.

SHARKSTOOTH PEAK, 12,462'

The violets in the mountains have broken the rocks.
— Tennessee Williams

Sharkstooth Peak's punishing reputation repels most hikers. It is climbed by a small percentage of adventurers who utilize its namesake trail and for good reason. Slithering, shattered, and unpredictable, this mountain is for list completers and courageous climbers who can't resist the magnetic pull of elemental, all-stone fierceness culminating in a remarkably sharp summit. Ultra steep slopes slide out from underfoot, holds are undependable, and self arrest is problematic. Navigation must be carefully deliberated and nuanced. Climb with no more than two or three sure-footed partners.

ABOUT THIS HIKE

Distance: 4.4 miles
Elevation Gain: 1,600 feet
Time: 3:00 to 4:30
Route Surface: trail, off-trail, steep scrambling, rockfall hazard, helmets recommended
Class: 3
Exposure: considerable
Navigation: challenging

Travel

Measure distance from the intersection of US 160 and CO 184 in Mancos. At the signal, turn north toward Dolores. In 0.3 mile, at the sign for Mancos State Park, turn right on Montezuma CR 42. At 5.5 miles, the road becomes FSR 561, West Mancos Road. Pass the Transfer Campground at 10.3 miles where pavement ends. Stay on FSR 561 at 11.1 miles. Pass the Aspen Guard Station at 11.9 miles. Turn right at mile 12.4 on FSR 350, Spruce Mill Road. It remains smooth and graded until mile 18.8. Turn on the right spur signed for the Twin Lakes and Sharkstooth trailheads, FSR 346. The next 1.5 miles require 4WD, good clearance, and sturdy tires. The track is rocky with potholes. There is dispersed camping along the road with ponds and a terrific view of Hesperus Mountain. One third of a mile before the trailhead, the road runs along the base of the Sharkstooth rock

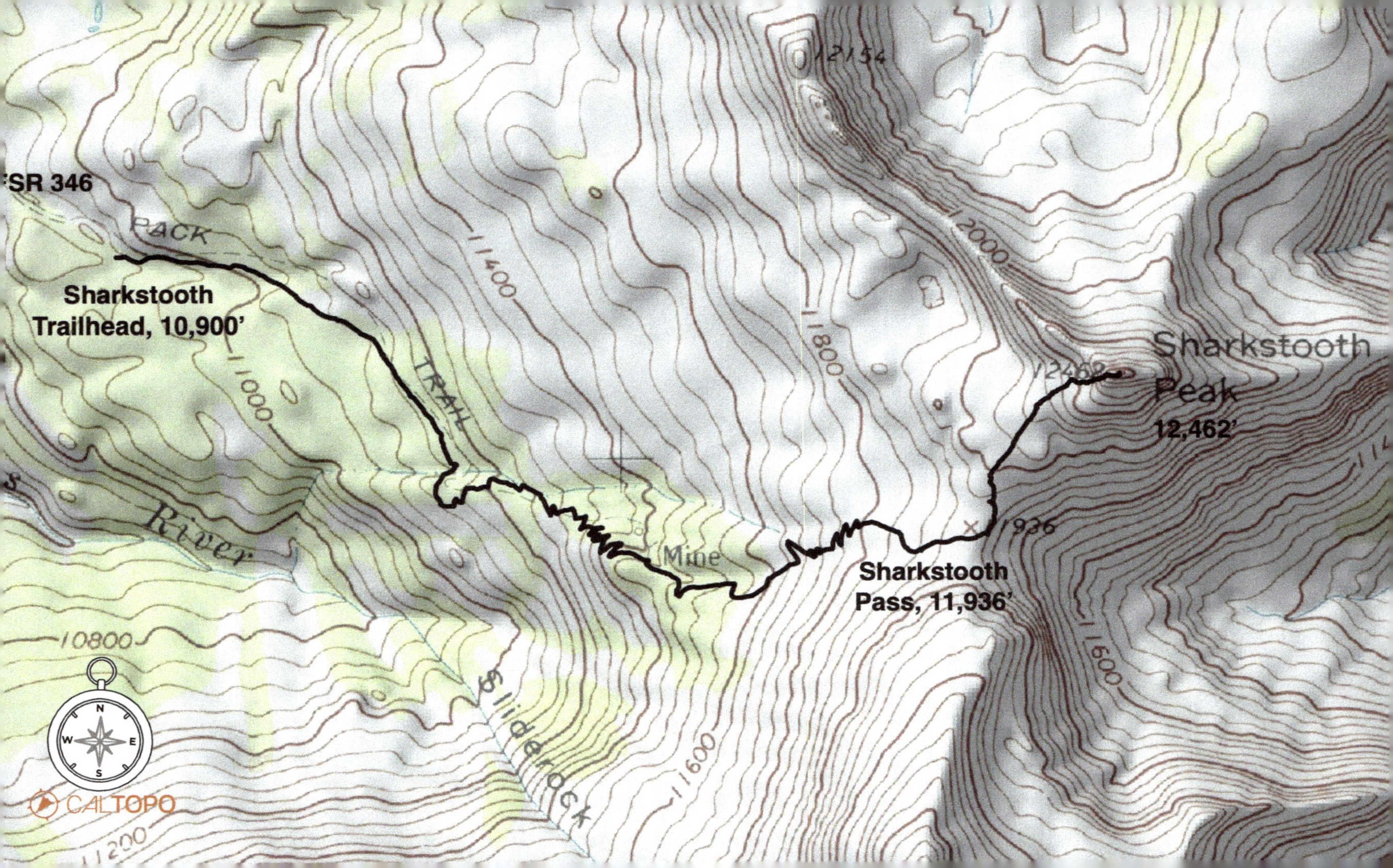
FSR 346
PACK
Sharkstooth Trailhead, 10,900'
TRAIL
River
Mine
Slidrock
Sharkstooth Pass, 11,936'
Sharkstooth Peak 12,462'
12,134
2000
1800
1400
1000
1100
10800
11200
11600
11600
936
CALTOPO

glacier. Park in a small lot at the end of the road, 20.3 miles from US 160.

Route

Sharkstooth Trail #620 is one of three trails that constitute the Mancos Spur. It connects the Western La Platas with the Highline Loop Recreation Trail and the Colorado Trail. The well-established pathway leaves from the east side of the parking lot at elevation 10,900 feet.

The trail skirts the southern runout of the Sharkstooth rock glacier. Picas forage amongst the rocks; a magnificent Colorado blue spruce holds back rolling stone. In mid-August, the woods foretell of impending autumn. Mushrooms sprout from the moist forest floor. Elderberries are even brighter than the crimson leaves of fireweed. Osha and delphinium transition from flower to seed. Cobalt blue bottle gentian, the harbinger of winter, presages the passage of summertime.

Cross a tributary of the North Fork of the Mancos River on a big, sturdy log at 0.8 mile. Hesperus Mountain, the tallest peak in the La Platas at 13,238 feet, is the banded, laidback triangular slab seen through a break in the timber.

Girdled by an ablative cliff-shield, even the grass finds no purchase on Sharkstooth.

At 11,650 feet, pass above treeline into the alpine tundra, a luminous landscape free of shadows. Switchbacks moderate the grade, our quarry comes into view, and the trail takes direct aim at the Sharkstooth/Centennial saddle.

Arrive on Sharkstooth Pass, 11,936', at 1.8 miles. Here we leave the Sharkstooth Trail which continues east to link up with the Colorado Trail at Taylor Lake near Kennebec Pass. For most hikers, the pass is a marker on their way to Centennial Peak, 13,062', just 0.8 mile south.

From the saddle, Sharkstooth Peak is a 526-foot climb over 0.4 mile. Most climbers will consume 1.5 to 2.5 hours, roundtrip. Resist the urge to barge up the south face. Yes, some people have been successful using this approach but it is more unstable than the recommended route.

To begin, head north on the softly rounded ridge until you have a direct shot at the west face of the mountain. The safest passage, and most likely the standard route if there is one, is to climb the shallow gully emanating from the notch just south of the apex. There are other conceivable routes but

they are a roll of the dice. The summit cone is a small, even intimate, space. Just to be sure about the best route, we spirited all over the west slope and even climbed 100 feet up the northwest ridge on the razorback of the rock glacier before getting cliffed out.

At 12,080 feet, the mountain bucks up but the slope is reasonably stable and doesn't get rigorously steep and loose until 12,200 feet. The fractured rock is poised at the angle of repose. It tends to settle in cresting waves—avoid disturbing them. The gravest danger is setting off a landslide above you. Navigation is a sustained puzzle. Make progress a dozen feet at a time, readjusting with micro route finding. Soft dirt passages are one clue you are on course.

Work your way up and into the gully, a debris slide path. The floor of the

trough is more stable than the splintered ribs on either side. There are a few good holds but most become dislodged when stepped on or pulled. Climb directly up the exposed Class 3 wall. There is no bypass. Then, climb through a chute that drains from the notch.

From the gap it is a short, straightforward walk to the zenith. Appropriately, the 4x5 foot fang is the smallest crest of any peak in the La Platas, a good part of its allure. The hard won vantage point has an incomparable view of three thirteeners: Centennial Peak, Lavender Peak, and Hesperus Mountain.

Swing visually from Lone Cone eastward to see the San Juans rippling off in the distance. Indian Trail Ridge, the skyway connector between the ranges, is across the Bear Creek Basin.

La Platas' largest rock glacier surges out in waves from the peak and northwest ridge. Burro Mountain, the most northerly ranked summit in the range is an extension of this ridge. Like Sharkstooth, it is a remnant of immensity, the structure that stood in this very place before the forces of erosion had their timeless way.

THE KNIFE:
WEST BABCOCK PEAK, 13,100'
TO SPILLER PEAK, 13,132'

You are what your deep driving desire is. As your desire is, so is your will.
As your will is, so is your deed. As your deed is, so is your destiny.

— The Upanishads

The La Plata Knife is a half-mile scramble across a serrated slice of stone. The traverse between West Babcock and Spiller peaks ranks among the finest in Colorado. The three-part trek is the most challenging, both physically and mentally, in the La Plata Mountains. Hike into Boren Creek Basin and mount a sustained, ultra-steep Class 3 pitch up the south face of West Babcock Peak. Exposure on the Knife is breathtaking and continuous; the crux is Class 4. Stone is fractured and friable on the south ridge of Spiller; holds are unreliable and exposure is considerable. Finish with a hardscrabble plunge back into the basin.

ABOUT THIS HIKE
Distance: 7.8 miles
Elevation Gain: 4,200 feet
Time: 6:00 to 9:00
Route Surface: jeep track, steep scrambling, gendarmes,
                         friable and loose rock, helmets recommended
Class: 4
Exposure: serious
Navigation: challenging

Travel

Measure distance from the junction of US 160 and La Plata Canyon Road, CR 124. After passing the hamlet of Mayday, the road turns to smooth dirt at 4.6 miles. Park in a pullout at 8.1 miles, just past Boren Creek.

Route

To West Babcock Peak

From the pullout, elevation 9,240 feet, walk up La Plata Canyon Road about 200 feet and head northwest up rocky Boren Creek Road, FSR 794.

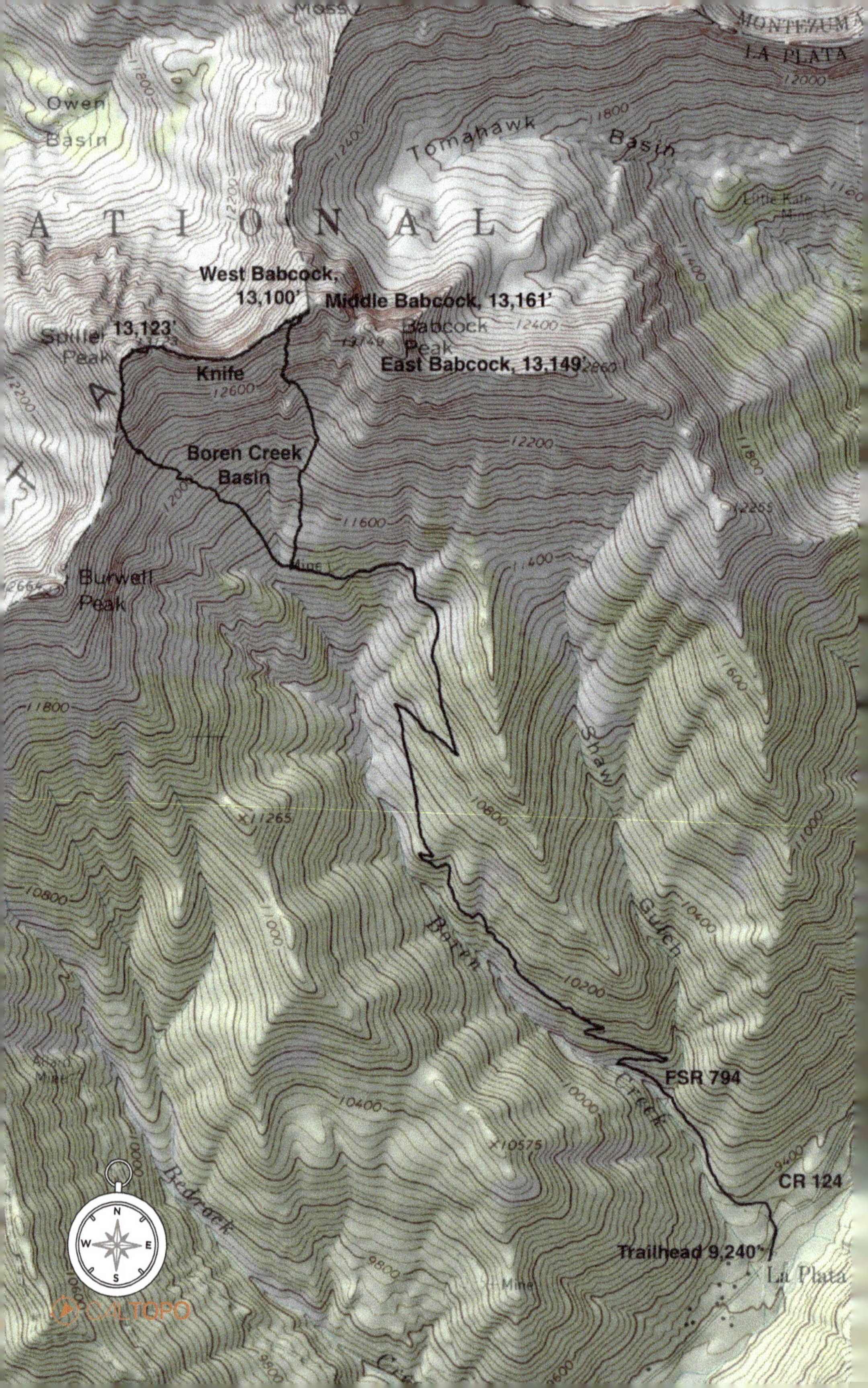

MOSS
MONTEZUMA
LA PLATA
12000
Owen
Basin
Tomahawk
Basin
Little Kate
Mine
A T I O N A L
West Babcock,
13,100'
Middle Babcock, 13,161'
Spiller Peak 13,123'
Babcock Peak
East Babcock, 13,149'
Knife
Boren Creek Basin
12600
12200
Burwell Peak
11800
X 11265
11800
Shaw Gulch
10800
11000
Boren
10800
FSR 794
Alard Mine
10400
X 10575
Bedrock
CR 124
1000
Trailhead 9,240'
La Plata
9800
Mine
CALTOPO
N
W   E
S

Cross Shaw Gulch at 0.5 mile. Ascending, the luminous aspen forest fades and dark timber takes a stand. At 1.7 miles, 10,480 feet, the route to Burwell Peak branches left. Stay on the main track to an abandoned mine on a gravity slope in the krummholz at 2.8 miles, 11,300 feet.

Begin the approach to West Babcock by passing to the right of the obvious orange outcrop below the cliffs (center-right).

Pause and take a moment to locate the proper route up West Babcock Peak. Five mountains encircle high-angle Boren Basin. Burwell Peak is the southern highpoint. From there, the rim points north to Spiller Peak and then it swings east. To the right of Spiller is the crux of the Knife at the "tooth." Next, is the south wall of the Knife, West Babcock with the smooth stone swale, Middle Babcock, and East Babcock. To confuse things, the La Plata quad labels East Babcock as Babcock Peak, 13,149'. And yet, Middle Babcock is the highest of the trio at 13,161 feet. It is the only ranked summit on the entire span.

There are two routes up West Babcock, the couloir route (just west of Middle Babcock) and the south face route, described here. While we have climbed both Middle and West Babcock from the gully, I do not recommend

this approach. Rocks are poised at the angle of repose and aggressively tumble when jostled. The rolling gash is on the move, the stones abraded on every facet. The Class 3 crux is covered in pebbles and slick dirt.

To get started on the south face route, climb north toward West Babcock, staying to the east of an orange outcrop studded with pyrite. The basin climb is rather tedious on a combination of grass, scree, talus, and boulders. It's just steep enough that much of the material shifts underfoot.

Note of Caution: We once witnessed two, three-foot cubes of stone cut loose from a Babcock couloir and, gathering more boulders, bounce-fly at 100 mph down the center of the basin where we had been moments prior. They skidded to a halt just shy of the jeep track. It was a narrow and lucky miss. Please be fully aware that your presence in the basin is potentially dangerous.

At about 12,160 feet you will come alongside a buttress, a dominant feature in the upper basin, an extension of West Babcock's south ridge. You have a choice. The easiest route continues up the talus slope, flanking the buttress on the east. Cut left on rust-colored stone and ascend to a small flat north of the buttress at 12,400 feet. To mount the exposed feature, zig and zag laterally to its south ridge. Scrambling is solid Class 3 on massive blocks with good holds. For some, this is the

Left: Possibly the ultimate challenge for La Plata aficionados, the Knife shows off its serrated blade after an early fall storm.

Photo by Forester Tesche

highlight of the entire adventure.

The alternate routes meet on the flat. A narrow, radically steep, 100-foot couloir extends northwest from the platform. This gully is the essential connector to a narrow section of ridge between snow-filled chutes and cliffs on both the east and west.

The climb pitches steeply from here to the summit with significant rock fall hazard for the next 700 vertical feet. Boulders on the couloir's floor are loose. Favor the walls where rock is more dependable. Still, some holds that appear well seated will pop off when disturbed. If you must use questionable holds, don't rely on them.

Once clear of the ravine, ascend the ridge a short distance on the west side. You will soon come to an opening where you may cross over to the east. There is considerable latitude in route possibilities from here. The west side isn't an option. A cliff-bound ravine holds snow deep into summer.

You may climb directly up the south rib, a Class 3 scramble. Or, more commonly, flank the blocky spine on the east by a few feet. If you wish, move further into the broad rock swale. The west side of the trough has some ledges with fairly good rock.

The upper mountain pitches ever more acutely. I have made contact with the west ridge of West Babcock in three different places. Traverse east to the summit, 3.6 miles, after 3,900 feet of vertical.

Among the big tops, on the north rim of Owen Basin is Hesperus Mountain, 13,238', the tallest peak in the range. Lone Cone is visible in the gap between Hesperus and the towers of Lavender Peak. The ridge spanning north to Mount Moss forms the divide between Tomahawk and Owen basins. It appears that if you got a running start you could leap over West Babcock's climbing couloir and land on Middle Babcock—alas, an illusion in this compact and complicated landscape. Look west to see the Knife slicing over to Spiller Peak on the divide between Owen and Boren basins. Sleeping Ute Mountain lies in repose in the distance.

The Knife

Helmets are recommended for the adrenaline-infused, half-mile traverse to Spiller Peak. Experienced scramblers will complete the span in about one hour, given optimum conditions and navigation choices. The Knife has a mixed reputation among the climbing community in Durango. There are horrific stories of people bailing from the ridge in desperation having been caught in electrical storms or encountering sheets of snow. Select a severe clear day for this crossing.

The half-mile traverse to Spiller is best approached on a day like this one.

Photo by Forester Tesche

To initiate, descend 140 feet. Some subsequent down-climbs are significantly steep, almost as challenging as the crux. It is best, as always, to follow the standard rule and stay pinned to the ridge. However, there are innumerable obstacles: snaggletooths, standing rocks, spires, and stacks. It will be clear whether to balance on top or defer a few feet to the north or south to bypass a gendarme.

Exposure begins right away and is sustained for the duration. The ridge varies from one slender block wide to a few feet. There is plenty of good rock, but a substantial share is loose and

Right: Making your way through this large chink in the ridge is the crux of the traverse.

Photo by Forester Tesche

unseated. Maintain concentration and test all your holds.

The crux is located about four-fifths of the way across the span. At a deeply incised declivity, work your way down unstable rubble into the notch. Cross the gap and locate the climbing wall a few feet north of center. The crux is a 15-foot, Class 4 pitch on good rock. Some climbers will appreciate a spot.

If you get caught in threatening weather or need to bail for any reason, it appears that you can down-climb into Boren Basin from the base of the crux. It won't be a pleasant descent and it is untested but the last time our group was in the notch it looked plausible.

Above the crux wall, the ridge is ridiculously steep and exposed. The grade relaxes and from there, it is a relatively simple but not trivial climb up the summit block. The hard-won zenith of Spiller Peak is spacious and welcoming. The mountain seems to thrive on the elation and deep satisfaction felt by climbers who have traveled from the east.

Spiller South Ridge to Boren Basin

Spiller is an ethereal apex, true. It is also the earthly pivot of Owen, Rush, and Boren basins. There is a winter climb from Owen Basin up the north-facing "Spiller Couloir." The final off-trail segment of this trek is the south ridge descent from Spiller Peak and the Boren Basin plunge. Please see the Spiller Peak (from Rush Basin) chapter for a description and images of the south ridge.

Maintain mindfulness on the south ridge social trail where rock is fractured, holds are unreliable, and exposure is considerable. There is some latitude in where you leave the ridge. Once we bailed too soon on what appeared to be a wildcat trail. That stranded us on resistant gravelly soil directly above a cliff. We clawed our way back to the ridgeline and continued down to a rocky couloir just north of the Spiller-Burwell saddle at 12,500 feet. Or, you may leave the ridge sooner after you have visually located "The Gate," a scree-slide weakness in a secondary cliff band.

The Boren Basin drop is a tedious 1,200-foot descent. There is some plunge-stepping and scree skiing mixed with large talus and resistant soil. For those of you who come through the gate, in mid-summer you will descend through a vibrant field of columbine. Close the loop at your launch point from the Boren Creek Road. Well dreamed. Well done.

Right: Hikers ascend the south ridge powered by pure joy.

Photo by Forester Tesche

ACKNOWLEDGEMENTS

Foremost, we are grateful to Debra's son, Forester Tesche, for climbing these peaks with us (starting with Centennial Peak at age ten), for making them all look easy, and for encouraging us to write this book...for his friends! Thank you, naturalist and stellar navigator John Bregar for answering our ceaseless questions about geology and botany; for introducing Debra to Lavender Peak and Mount Moss on a cold day in November of 2007; and for ably guiding her across The Knife. Thank you, Steve Allen, for your friendship, encouragement, and belief in this project from its inception. Historian Robert McDaniel provided us with resources on the early days of mining in the La Platas and linked us with the Animas Museum, one of our photograph repositories.

Jennifer Sanchez helped us with rare photo collections at the University of Colorado Boulder Libraries. Katie Sauter of the library staff of The American Alpine Club helped us with the history of some of the La Plata place names and provided the invaluable reference to Jennifer Runyon of the research staff of the U.S. Board on Geographic Names, who located and scanned a number of original documents in their collection.

We wish to thank the professionals who worked with us for four years to produce this book: editor Elizabeth A. Green with The Write Connection in Bayfield, Colorado; and book designer Lisa Snider in Portland, Oregon. This book never would have become a reality without their expertise.

We have a large group of friends who have climbed and reclimbed these routes with us over the years. For their unwavering enthusiasm for the La Platas, competency in the backcountry, and for having our backs, our heartfelt thanks go out to: Jeff Bailey, Charlie Berglund, Chris Blackshear, John Bregar, Rich and Betsey Butler, Lynn Coburn, Lyle Hancock, KT and Arthur Howard, Judy Mack, Dave Peters, Jodie Petersen, Janna Ranson, Sherry Suenram, Bob Thompson, Travis Ward, and Carolyn Wilber.

The following institutions and websites supported our efforts: American Alpine Club; Animas Museum; Center of Southwest Studies at Fort Lewis College; Durango Public Library; Library of Congress; University of Colorado Boulder Libraries Rare Collections; Navajo People-The Diné, http://navajopeople.org; Al Schneider with https://www.swcoloradowildflowers.com; and David Lavender's granddaughter Sarah Lavender with https://sarahrunning.substack.com.

The following publications were integral to our project:

Eckel, Edwin B., et al. *Geology and Ore Deposits of the La Plata District, Colorado.* United States Government Printing Office, Washington, 1949.

Griffiths, Thomas Melvin. *San Juan Country.* Pruett, Boulder, CO, 1984.

Hayden, F. V. *Ninth Annual Report of the United States Geological and Geographical Survey of the Territories Embracing Colorado and Parts of Adjacent Territories: Report of Progress of the Exploration for the Year 1875.* Government Printing Office, Washington, 1877.

Geological And Geographical Survey Of The Territories, F. V. Hayden. *Geological and geographical atlas of Colorado and portions of adjacent territory.* [New York J. Bien, lith, 1877] Map.

Lavender, David. *One Man's West.* Bison Press, Lincoln, NE, 2007.

Lavender, Dwight G., Thomas Melvin Griffiths & Carleton Curtis Long. *The San Juan Mountaineers' Climber's Guide to Southwestern Colorado.* Colorado Mountain Club, Golden, CO, 2008, out of print.

Peel, John, & Paul Pixler. *Hiking Trails of Southwestern Colorado, Fifth Edition.* West Margin Press, Berkeley, CA, 2020.

Seyfarth, Jill, & Ruth Lambert. *Pioneers, Prospectors and Trout: A Historic Context for La Plata County, Colorado.* La Plata County Planning Department, 2010.

Smith, Duane A., *Song of the Hammer and Drill: The Colorado San Juans, 1860-1914.* University Press of Colorado, Boulder, 2000.

ABOUT THE AUTHORS

Debra Van Winegarden has been hiking wild landscapes her entire life. As a child, she camped in Yosemite every summer and climbed Half Dome at age fourteen. Each year she went on eight-day, eighty-mile backpacks in the Sierra Nevada with her family. The discipline of recording field notes led naturally to publishing 80 hiking columns in *The Durango Herald*. Her desire to document our ever-changing planet is manifest in her blog, Earthline: The American West, established in 2014. Debra wrote the hiking descriptions for this guidebook.

Photo by Lynn Coburn

The authors on the high point of the La Plata Mountains.

Professionally, Debra was an environmental science and patent law librarian (MA, University of California, Berkeley). Following that, she earned a Masters in Counseling Psychology and established a therapeutic practice. She had the most fun driving crowded ski buses in treacherous conditions in Crested Butte. Debra lives in Durango.

Thomas Holt Ward has been an amateur photographer since he converted the family's downstairs half-bath into a darkroom at age twelve. He was also the earliest of adopters in digital photography and wrote his own digital image processing programs before any were commercially available. After discovering hiking and backpacking in college, exploring wilderness became another life-long pursuit. After meeting Debra, his computer skills were instrumental in setting up and maintaining her blog while also accompanying her on their shared adventures. His trusty battle-hardened Jeep has also provided access to the most remote of trailheads. Thomas wrote the introductory chapters and the photo captions for this guidebook.

Professionally, Thomas was a computer programmer throughout his life, specializing in real-time device drivers. He holds a BA in Linguistics from Pomona College in Clairemont, CA.

INDEX

Italicized page numbers indicate photographs

A

alpine xxii
arborglyphs *94*
arctic gentian *20*
aspen xxiii
Aspen Loop Trail 26

B

Baker Peak 67, *68*, 69–71, 78
      Point 11,818' 72
      Point 11,900' 69
Bald Knob 61–65
      Point 11,391 64
      Point 11,670' 65
      Point 11,900' 64
Baldy Peak 101–106
      Point 8,980' 105
Barnroof Point 103
Bashō, Matsuo 9
Basin Creek 121
Bear Creek Basin 16–*19*
Bear Creek Pass 16, *17*, 18
Bear Creek Trail 18
Bedrock Creek OHV Trail 93
Bessie G Mine 150
Big Stick Ditch 105
Boren Creek Basin 97, 131, 157
Boren Creek *97*
Boren Creek Road 95, 157
Burro Benchmark 21
Burro Mountain 21–*26*
      Peak 11,580' 24
      Point 11,454' 23
      Point 11,553' 24
      Windy Gap 23

Burroughs, John 21
Burwell Peak xxix, 92, *95*, 98, 99

C

Centennial Peak *17*, 18, 49–53
Chief Ignacio xxvii
Colorado Trail 4, 9, 15, 16, 27, 36
columbine *59*
Columbine Hill 57
Columbus Basin 143, *146*
cornhusk lillies *88*
Cumberland Mountain 27–33
Cutler Formation 38

D

Dalla, Herman 29
Deadwood Mountain 73, 75, 79
Deep Creek 103
Deep Creek Trailhead 103
Diorite Peak 55, 57, 59
Dry Fork 103
Durango *77*

E

Eagle Pass 64, 147, 150
early westerners xxvi
East Babcock Peak 127, 128, *129*
      Point 12,860' 129
East Mancos River 140
Edwards, Ralph 35
elegant death camas *50*, 51
Ellingwood, Albert R. xxix
Engelmann spruce *30*

G

Geology xix, xx, xxi
Gibbs Peak xxix, 87, *91*, 92
Gibbs Road 93
glacier lily *10*
Goethe 95
Gold King Mill 71
Gold King Mine 62
Govinda, Lama 73
Graham, Stephen 15
Green Bus Trail 89
Griffiths, Thomas Melvin (Mel) xxx

H

Hayden Expedition xix, xxviii, xxix
Hayden, F.V. xxviii
heartleaf arnica *24*
Helmet Peak 41–43
Hesperus Mountain *xxi*, 5, 20, 50,
    111–116
      Point 11,891' 113
Historic Highline Loop 6, 15, 18
Hogan, Linda 41
Hogback, the 42, 43
Holmes, William H. xix
human history xxv–xxix

I

Indian Trail Ridge 3–6, 16
    Boulder Playground 6
    Peak 12,338' 4
    Point 12,181 *4*
    Point 12,258' *4*

J

Johnson, Trebbe 111

K

Keller, Helen 119
Kennebec Pass 10, 11, *13*, 33, 36
Kennebec Pass Trailhead 9, 15, 27,
    36, 150
Kennebec Peak 9–11, *13*, 33
    Peak 12,101' 9
Kerouac, Jack 61
Kiabab Mine 83
Kipling, Rudyard 87
Knife, the 157, 159, *160*, 163, 166

L

La Plata City 73
La Plata Mountains laccolith 52, 114
La Plata Mountains *5*, 11
La Plata River 62, 68, 75
Lavender Peak 119, *120*, 123–*125*
Lavender, Dwight xxix, *xxx*
Lewis Creek 62
Lewis Creek Road 62, 68
Lewis Mountain 31, 143, *145*, 1
    47, 150
life zones xxi, xxii
    alpine xxii
    montane xxii
    subalpine xxii
Lightner Creek 103
Little Kate Mine 57, 121, 128
Little, Olga 35, *39*
Long, Carleton xxx

M

Macfarlane, Robert 67
Madden Creek Trail 93, 94
Madden Peak 81, 82, *84*, 87, 89
Mallory, George Leigh 131
Messner, Reinhold xvi

Michelangelo 127
Middle Babcock Peak 131, 133, *134*, 136-137
Miner's Cabin Trail 88
mining xxvii, xxviii
montane xxii
Moss, John *xxvii*, xxviii
Mount Moss xxviii, 59, 119, *120*, 121–125
Muldoon Mine 27, 29

N
Nachmann, Rabbi 143
Native Americans xxvi
Navajo 111
Neptune Creek 75
Notch, the 12, 150

O
Ohwiler Ridge 75
Olga Little Mountain 35, *36*–39
Oliver, Mary 139
Osho 55

P
Parrott City xxvii
Parrott Peak 81–*85*, 87, 89
Parrott, Tiburcio xxvii
Perins Peak State Wildlife Area 101, 103
Point Lookout 43
prehistoric inhabitants xxv
Public Lands xxxi
Puzzle Mine 69
Puzzle Pass 69

Q
queen's crown *10*

R
recreational use xxviii, xxix, xxx
Rivera, Juan Maria Antonia xxvi
Roosevelt, Theodore xxxi
Root Creek *88*
Rush Basin 41, 43, *44*, 140, *141*
　　Point 11,490' 43
　　Point 11,522' 44
　　Point 12,201' 44

S
San Juan National Forest xxxi, 101
Sharkstooth Pass 17, 154
Sharkstooth Peak *17*, *20*, 151–156
Sharkstooth Trail 6, 15–20, 49, 50, *153*
　　Point 12,117' 17
Shaw Gulch 95
Silver Mountain 67–*76*, 77, 78
Silver Mountain Traverse 71
Sleeping Ute Mountain 43, *82*
Sliderock Trail *13*, 29, *31*
Snowstorm Peak 143, 145, 146, 150
　　Point 12,420' 146
Spiller Peak 139–*142*, 157, 166
　　Point 12,201' 140
spotted coral root *107*
Star Peak 87, 90
　　Peak 11,870' *90*
　　Point 11,672' 90
　　Point 11,931' 91
Starvation Creek 85
subalpine xxii

T
Tagore, Rabindranath 27
Taylor Lake 4, 16
Texas Chief Mine 105

Thoreau, Henry David 49
Tirbircio Creek 71, 79
Tolkien, J.R.R. 3
Tomahawk Basin 55, 121, 127
Tomahawk Mining Company 57, 121
Tundra xxiv

U
Upanishads, The 157

V
vegetation xxiii, xxiv, xxv

W
West Babcock Peak 157, *161*
West Mancos Trail 112, 113
wildflowers xxiv
wildlife xxii
Williams, Tennessee 151
Windy Gap 25
Windy Williams Mill 53
Wordsworth, William 101

Y
Yeats, W.B. 81